Microsoft®
Training &
Certification

2276B: Implementing a Microsoft® Windows® Server 2003 Network Infrastructure: Network Hosts

route print

Dec 1,2 2005

Released: 05/2003

Microsoft®

Course Number: 2276B
Part Number: X10-00823
Released: 05/2003

END-USER LICENSE AGREEMENT FOR MICROSOFT OFFICIAL CURRICULUM COURSEWARE –STUDENT EDITION

PLEASE READ THIS END-USER LICENSE AGREEMENT ("EULA") CAREFULLY. BY USING THE MATERIALS AND/OR USING OR INSTALLING THE SOFTWARE THAT ACCOMPANIES THIS EULA (COLLECTIVELY, THE "LICENSED CONTENT"), YOU AGREE TO THE TERMS OF THIS EULA. IF YOU DO NOT AGREE, DO NOT USE THE LICENSED CONTENT.

1. **GENERAL.** This EULA is a legal agreement between you (either an individual or a single entity) and Microsoft Corporation ("Microsoft"). This EULA governs the Licensed Content, which includes computer software (including online and electronic documentation), training materials, and any other associated media and printed materials. This EULA applies to updates, supplements, add-on components, and Internet-based services components of the Licensed Content that Microsoft may provide or make available to you unless Microsoft provides other terms with the update, supplement, add-on component, or Internet-based services component. Microsoft reserves the right to discontinue any Internet-based services provided to you or made available to you through the use of the Licensed Content. This EULA also governs any product support services relating to the Licensed Content except as may be included in another agreement between you and Microsoft. An amendment or addendum to this EULA may accompany the Licensed Content.

2. **GENERAL GRANT OF LICENSE.** Microsoft grants you the following rights, conditioned on your compliance with all the terms and conditions of this EULA. Microsoft grants you a limited, non-exclusive, royalty-free license to install and use the Licensed Content solely in conjunction with your participation as a student in an Authorized Training Session (as defined below). You may install and use one copy of the software on a single computer, device, workstation, terminal, or other digital electronic or analog device ("Device"). You may make a second copy of the software and install it on a portable Device for the exclusive use of the person who is the primary user of the first copy of the software. A license for the software may not be shared for use by multiple end users. An "Authorized Training Session" means a training session conducted at a Microsoft Certified Technical Education Center, an IT Academy, via a Microsoft Certified Partner, or such other entity as Microsoft may designate from time to time in writing, by a Microsoft Certified Trainer (for more information on these entities, please visit www.microsoft.com). WITHOUT LIMITING THE FOREGOING, COPYING OR REPRODUCTION OF THE LICENSED CONTENT TO ANY SERVER OR LOCATION FOR FURTHER REPRODUCTION OR REDISTRIBUTION IS EXPRESSLY PROHIBITED.

3. **DESCRIPTION OF OTHER RIGHTS AND LICENSE LIMITATIONS**

    3.1 *Use of Documentation and Printed Training Materials.*

    3.1.1 The documents and related graphics included in the Licensed Content may include technical inaccuracies or typographical errors. Changes are periodically made to the content. Microsoft may make improvements and/or changes in any of the components of the Licensed Content at any time without notice. The names of companies, products, people, characters and/or data mentioned in the Licensed Content may be fictitious and are in no way intended to represent any real individual, company, product or event, unless otherwise noted.

    3.1.2 Microsoft grants you the right to reproduce portions of documents (such as student workbooks, white papers, press releases, datasheets and FAQs) (the "Documents") provided with the Licensed Content. You may not print any book (either electronic or print version) in its entirety. If you choose to reproduce Documents, you agree that: (a) use of such printed Documents will be solely in conjunction with your personal training use; (b) the Documents will not republished or posted on any network computer or broadcast in any media; (c) any reproduction will include either the Document's original copyright notice or a copyright notice to Microsoft's benefit substantially in the format provided below; and (d) to comply with all terms and conditions of this EULA. In addition, no modifications may made to any Document.

    Form of Notice:

    © 2003. Reprinted with permission by Microsoft Corporation. All rights reserved.

    Microsoft and Windows are either registered trademarks or trademarks of Microsoft Corporation in the US and/or other countries. Other product and company names mentioned herein may be the trademarks of their respective owners.

    3.2 *Use of Media Elements.* The Licensed Content may include certain photographs, clip art, animations, sounds, music, and video clips (together "Media Elements"). You may not modify these Media Elements.

    3.3 *Use of Sample Code.* In the event that the Licensed Content includes sample code in source or object format ("Sample Code"), Microsoft grants you a limited, non-exclusive, royalty-free license to use, copy and modify the Sample Code; if you elect to exercise the foregoing rights, you agree to comply with all other terms and conditions of this EULA, including without limitation Sections 3.4, 3.5, and 6.

    3.4 *Permitted Modifications.* In the event that you exercise any rights provided under this EULA to create modifications of the Licensed Content, you agree that any such modifications: (a) will not be used for providing training where a fee is charged in public or private classes; (b) indemnify, hold harmless, and defend Microsoft from and against any claims or lawsuits, including attorneys' fees, which arise from or result from your use of any modified version of the Licensed Content; and (c) not to transfer or assign any rights to any modified version of the Licensed Content to any third party without the express written permission of Microsoft.

3.5   *Reproduction/Redistribution Licensed Content.* Except as expressly provided in this EULA, you may not reproduce or distribute the Licensed Content or any portion thereof (including any permitted modifications) to any third parties without the express written permission of Microsoft.

4.   **RESERVATION OF RIGHTS AND OWNERSHIP.** Microsoft reserves all rights not expressly granted to you in this EULA. The Licensed Content is protected by copyright and other intellectual property laws and treaties. Microsoft or its suppliers own the title, copyright, and other intellectual property rights in the Licensed Content. You may not remove or obscure any copyright, trademark or patent notices that appear on the Licensed Content, or any components thereof, as delivered to you. **The Licensed Content is licensed, not sold.**

5.   **LIMITATIONS ON REVERSE ENGINEERING, DECOMPILATION, AND DISASSEMBLY.** You may not reverse engineer, decompile, or disassemble the Software or Media Elements, except and only to the extent that such activity is expressly permitted by applicable law notwithstanding this limitation.

6.   **LIMITATIONS ON SALE, RENTAL, ETC. AND CERTAIN ASSIGNMENTS.** You may not provide commercial hosting services with, sell, rent, lease, lend, sublicense, or assign copies of the Licensed Content, or any portion thereof (including any permitted modifications thereof) on a stand-alone basis or as part of any collection, product or service.

7.   **CONSENT TO USE OF DATA.** You agree that Microsoft and its affiliates may collect and use technical information gathered as part of the product support services provided to you, if any, related to the Licensed Content. Microsoft may use this information solely to improve our products or to provide customized services or technologies to you and will not disclose this information in a form that personally identifies you.

8.   **LINKS TO THIRD PARTY SITES.** You may link to third party sites through the use of the Licensed Content. The third party sites are not under the control of Microsoft, and Microsoft is not responsible for the contents of any third party sites, any links contained in third party sites, or any changes or updates to third party sites. Microsoft is not responsible for webcasting or any other form of transmission received from any third party sites. Microsoft is providing these links to third party sites to you only as a convenience, and the inclusion of any link does not imply an endorsement by Microsoft of the third party site.

9.   **ADDITIONAL LICENSED CONTENT/SERVICES.** This EULA applies to updates, supplements, add-on components, or Internet-based services components, of the Licensed Content that Microsoft may provide to you or make available to you after the date you obtain your initial copy of the Licensed Content, unless we provide other terms along with the update, supplement, add-on component, or Internet-based services component. Microsoft reserves the right to discontinue any Internet-based services provided to you or made available to you through the use of the Licensed Content.

10.   **U.S. GOVERNMENT LICENSE RIGHTS.** All software provided to the U.S. Government pursuant to solicitations issued on or after December 1, 1995 is provided with the commercial license rights and restrictions described elsewhere herein. All software provided to the U.S. Government pursuant to solicitations issued prior to December 1, 1995 is provided with "Restricted Rights" as provided for in FAR, 48 CFR 52.227-14 (JUNE 1987) or DFAR, 48 CFR 252.227-7013 (OCT 1988), as applicable.

11.   **EXPORT RESTRICTIONS.** You acknowledge that the Licensed Content is subject to U.S. export jurisdiction. You agree to comply with all applicable international and national laws that apply to the Licensed Content, including the U.S. Export Administration Regulations, as well as end-user, end-use, and destination restrictions issued by U.S. and other governments. For additional information see <http://www.microsoft.com/exporting/>.

12.   **TRANSFER.** The initial user of the Licensed Content may make a one-time permanent transfer of this EULA and Licensed Content to another end user, provided the initial user retains no copies of the Licensed Content. The transfer may not be an indirect transfer, such as a consignment. Prior to the transfer, the end user receiving the Licensed Content must agree to all the EULA terms.

13.   **"NOT FOR RESALE" LICENSED CONTENT.** Licensed Content identified as "Not For Resale" or "NFR," may not be sold or otherwise transferred for value, or used for any purpose other than demonstration, test or evaluation.

14.   **TERMINATION.** Without prejudice to any other rights, Microsoft may terminate this EULA if you fail to comply with the terms and conditions of this EULA. In such event, you must destroy all copies of the Licensed Content and all of its component parts.

15.   <u>**DISCLAIMER OF WARRANTIES.**</u> **TO THE MAXIMUM EXTENT PERMITTED BY APPLICABLE LAW, MICROSOFT AND ITS SUPPLIERS PROVIDE THE LICENSED CONTENT AND SUPPORT SERVICES (IF ANY)** *AS IS AND WITH ALL FAULTS,* **AND MICROSOFT AND ITS SUPPLIERS HEREBY DISCLAIM ALL OTHER WARRANTIES AND CONDITIONS, WHETHER EXPRESS, IMPLIED OR STATUTORY, INCLUDING, BUT NOT LIMITED TO, ANY (IF ANY) IMPLIED WARRANTIES, DUTIES OR CONDITIONS OF MERCHANTABILITY, OF FITNESS FOR A PARTICULAR PURPOSE, OF RELIABILITY OR AVAILABILITY, OF ACCURACY OR COMPLETENESS OF RESPONSES, OF RESULTS, OF WORKMANLIKE EFFORT, OF LACK OF VIRUSES, AND OF LACK OF NEGLIGENCE, ALL WITH REGARD TO THE LICENSED CONTENT, AND THE PROVISION OF OR FAILURE TO PROVIDE SUPPORT OR OTHER SERVICES, INFORMATION, SOFTWARE, AND RELATED CONTENT THROUGH THE LICENSED CONTENT, OR OTHERWISE ARISING OUT OF THE USE OF THE LICENSED CONTENT. ALSO, THERE IS NO WARRANTY OR CONDITION OF TITLE, QUIET ENJOYMENT, QUIET POSSESSION, CORRESPONDENCE TO DESCRIPTION OR NON-INFRINGEMENT WITH REGARD TO THE LICENSED CONTENT. THE ENTIRE RISK AS TO THE QUALITY, OR ARISING OUT OF THE USE OR PERFORMANCE OF THE LICENSED CONTENT, AND ANY SUPPORT SERVICES, REMAINS WITH YOU.**

16.   <u>**EXCLUSION OF INCIDENTAL, CONSEQUENTIAL AND CERTAIN OTHER DAMAGES.**</u> **TO THE MAXIMUM EXTENT PERMITTED BY APPLICABLE LAW, IN NO EVENT SHALL MICROSOFT OR ITS SUPPLIERS BE LIABLE FOR ANY SPECIAL, INCIDENTAL, PUNITIVE, INDIRECT, OR CONSEQUENTIAL DAMAGES WHATSOEVER (INCLUDING, BUT NOT**

LIMITED TO, DAMAGES FOR LOSS OF PROFITS OR CONFIDENTIAL OR OTHER INFORMATION, FOR BUSINESS INTERRUPTION, FOR PERSONAL INJURY, FOR LOSS OF PRIVACY, FOR FAILURE TO MEET ANY DUTY INCLUDING OF GOOD FAITH OR OF REASONABLE CARE, FOR NEGLIGENCE, AND FOR ANY OTHER PECUNIARY OR OTHER LOSS WHATSOEVER) ARISING OUT OF OR IN ANY WAY RELATED TO THE USE OF OR INABILITY TO USE THE LICENSED CONTENT, THE PROVISION OF OR FAILURE TO PROVIDE SUPPORT OR OTHER SERVICES, INFORMATION, SOFTWARE, AND RELATED CONTENT THROUGH THE LICENSED CONTENT, OR OTHERWISE ARISING OUT OF THE USE OF THE LICENSED CONTENT, OR OTHERWISE UNDER OR IN CONNECTION WITH ANY PROVISION OF THIS EULA, EVEN IN THE EVENT OF THE FAULT, TORT (INCLUDING NEGLIGENCE), MISREPRESENTATION, STRICT LIABILITY, BREACH OF CONTRACT OR BREACH OF WARRANTY OF MICROSOFT OR ANY SUPPLIER, AND EVEN IF MICROSOFT OR ANY SUPPLIER HAS BEEN ADVISED OF THE POSSIBILITY OF SUCH DAMAGES. BECAUSE SOME STATES/JURISDICTIONS DO NOT ALLOW THE EXCLUSION OR LIMITATION OF LIABILITY FOR CONSEQUENTIAL OR INCIDENTAL DAMAGES, THE ABOVE LIMITATION MAY NOT APPLY TO YOU.

17.   <u>LIMITATION OF LIABILITY AND REMEDIES.</u> NOTWITHSTANDING ANY DAMAGES THAT YOU MIGHT INCUR FOR ANY REASON WHATSOEVER (INCLUDING, WITHOUT LIMITATION, ALL DAMAGES REFERENCED HEREIN AND ALL DIRECT OR GENERAL DAMAGES IN CONTRACT OR ANYTHING ELSE), THE ENTIRE LIABILITY OF MICROSOFT AND ANY OF ITS SUPPLIERS UNDER ANY PROVISION OF THIS EULA AND YOUR EXCLUSIVE REMEDY HEREUNDER SHALL BE LIMITED TO THE GREATER OF THE ACTUAL DAMAGES YOU INCUR IN REASONABLE RELIANCE ON THE LICENSED CONTENT UP TO THE AMOUNT ACTUALLY PAID BY YOU FOR THE LICENSED CONTENT OR US$5.00. THE FOREGOING LIMITATIONS, EXCLUSIONS AND DISCLAIMERS SHALL APPLY TO THE MAXIMUM EXTENT PERMITTED BY APPLICABLE LAW, EVEN IF ANY REMEDY FAILS ITS ESSENTIAL PURPOSE.

18.   **APPLICABLE LAW.** If you acquired this Licensed Content in the United States, this EULA is governed by the laws of the State of Washington. If you acquired this Licensed Content in Canada, unless expressly prohibited by local law, this EULA is governed by the laws in force in the Province of Ontario, Canada; and, in respect of any dispute which may arise hereunder, you consent to the jurisdiction of the federal and provincial courts sitting in Toronto, Ontario. If you acquired this Licensed Content in the European Union, Iceland, Norway, or Switzerland, then local law applies. If you acquired this Licensed Content in any other country, then local law may apply.

19.   **ENTIRE AGREEMENT; SEVERABILITY.** This EULA (including any addendum or amendment to this EULA which is included with the Licensed Content) are the entire agreement between you and Microsoft relating to the Licensed Content and the support services (if any) and they supersede all prior or contemporaneous oral or written communications, proposals and representations with respect to the Licensed Content or any other subject matter covered by this EULA. To the extent the terms of any Microsoft policies or programs for support services conflict with the terms of this EULA, the terms of this EULA shall control. If any provision of this EULA is held to be void, invalid, unenforceable or illegal, the other provisions shall continue in full force and effect.

Should you have any questions concerning this EULA, or if you desire to contact Microsoft for any reason, please use the address information enclosed in this Licensed Content to contact the Microsoft subsidiary serving your country or visit Microsoft on the World Wide Web at http://www.microsoft.com.

Si vous avez acquis votre Contenu Sous Licence Microsoft au CANADA :

DÉNI DE GARANTIES. Dans la mesure maximale permise par les lois applicables, le Contenu Sous Licence et les services de soutien technique (le cas échéant) sont fournis *TELS QUELS ET AVEC TOUS LES DÉFAUTS* par Microsoft et ses fournisseurs, lesquels par les présentes dénient toutes autres garanties et conditions expresses, implicites ou en vertu de la loi, notamment, mais sans limitation, (le cas échéant) les garanties, devoirs ou conditions implicites de qualité marchande, d'adaptation à une fin usage particulière, de fiabilité ou de disponibilité, d'exactitude ou d'exhaustivité des réponses, des résultats, des efforts déployés selon les règles de l'art, d'absence de virus et d'absence de négligence, le tout à l'égard du Contenu Sous Licence et de la prestation des services de soutien technique ou de l'omission de la 'une telle prestation des services de soutien technique ou à l'égard de la fourniture ou de l'omission de la fourniture de tous autres services, renseignements, Contenus Sous Licence, et contenu qui s'y rapporte grâce au Contenu Sous Licence ou provenant autrement de l'utilisation du Contenu Sous Licence. PAR AILLEURS, IL N'Y A AUCUNE GARANTIE OU CONDITION QUANT AU TITRE DE PROPRIÉTÉ, À LA JOUISSANCE OU LA POSSESSION PAISIBLE, À LA CONCORDANCE À UNE DESCRIPTION NI QUANT À UNE ABSENCE DE CONTREFAÇON CONCERNANT LE CONTENU SOUS LICENCE.

<u>EXCLUSION DES DOMMAGES ACCESSOIRES, INDIRECTS ET DE CERTAINS AUTRES DOMMAGES.</u> DANS LA MESURE MAXIMALE PERMISE PAR LES LOIS APPLICABLES, EN AUCUN CAS MICROSOFT OU SES FOURNISSEURS NE SERONT RESPONSABLES DES DOMMAGES SPÉCIAUX, CONSÉCUTIFS, ACCESSOIRES OU INDIRECTS DE QUELQUE NATURE QUE CE SOIT (NOTAMMENT, LES DOMMAGES À L'ÉGARD DU MANQUE À GAGNER OU DE LA DIVULGATION DE RENSEIGNEMENTS CONFIDENTIELS OU AUTRES, DE LA PERTE D'EXPLOITATION, DE BLESSURES CORPORELLES, DE LA VIOLATION DE LA VIE PRIVÉE, DE L'OMISSION DE REMPLIR TOUT DEVOIR, Y COMPRIS D'AGIR DE BONNE FOI OU D'EXERCER UN SOIN RAISONNABLE, DE LA NÉGLIGENCE ET DE TOUTE AUTRE PERTE PÉCUNIAIRE OU AUTRE PERTE

DE QUELQUE NATURE QUE CE SOIT) SE RAPPORTE DE QUELQUE MANIÈRE QUE CE SOIT À L'UTILISATION DU CONTENU SOUS LICENCE OU À L'INCAPACITÉ DE S'EN SERVIR, À LA PRESTATION OU À L'OMISSION DE LA 'UNE TELLE PRESTATION DE SERVICES DE SOUTIEN TECHNIQUE OU À LA FOURNITURE OU À L'OMISSION DE LA FOURNITURE DE TOUS AUTRES SERVICES, RENSEIGNEMENTS, CONTENUS SOUS LICENCE, ET CONTENU QUI S'Y RAPPORTE GRÂCE AU CONTENU SOUS LICENCE OU PROVENANT AUTREMENT DE L'UTILISATION DU CONTENU SOUS LICENCE OU AUTREMENT AUX TERMES DE TOUTE DISPOSITION DE LA U PRÉSENTE CONVENTION EULA OU RELATIVEMENT À UNE TELLE DISPOSITION, MÊME EN CAS DE FAUTE, DE DÉLIT CIVIL (Y COMPRIS LA NÉGLIGENCE), DE RESPONSABILITÉ STRICTE, DE VIOLATION DE CONTRAT OU DE VIOLATION DE GARANTIE DE MICROSOFT OU DE TOUT FOURNISSEUR ET MÊME SI MICROSOFT OU TOUT FOURNISSEUR A ÉTÉ AVISÉ DE LA POSSIBILITÉ DE TELS DOMMAGES.

<u>LIMITATION DE RESPONSABILITÉ ET RECOURS.</u>   MALGRÉ LES DOMMAGES QUE VOUS PUISSIEZ SUBIR POUR QUELQUE MOTIF QUE CE SOIT (NOTAMMENT, MAIS SANS LIMITATION, TOUS LES DOMMAGES SUSMENTIONNÉS ET TOUS LES DOMMAGES DIRECTS OU GÉNÉRAUX OU AUTRES), LA SEULE RESPONSABILITÉ 'OBLIGATION INTÉGRALE DE MICROSOFT ET DE L'UN OU L'AUTRE DE SES FOURNISSEURS AUX TERMES DE TOUTE DISPOSITION DEU LA PRÉSENTE CONVENTION EULA ET VOTRE RECOURS EXCLUSIF À L'ÉGARD DE TOUT CE QUI PRÉCÈDE SE LIMITE AU PLUS ÉLEVÉ ENTRE LES MONTANTS SUIVANTS : LE MONTANT QUE VOUS AVEZ RÉELLEMENT PAYÉ POUR LE CONTENU SOUS LICENCE OU 5,00 $US. LES LIMITES, EXCLUSIONS ET DÉNIS QUI PRÉCÈDENT (Y COMPRIS LES CLAUSES CI-DESSUS), S'APPLIQUENT DANS LA MESURE MAXIMALE PERMISE PAR LES LOIS APPLICABLES, MÊME SI TOUT RECOURS N'ATTEINT PAS SON BUT ESSENTIEL.

À moins que cela ne soit prohibé par le droit local applicable, la présente Convention est régie par les lois de la province d'Ontario, Canada. Vous consentez Chacune des parties à la présente reconnaît irrévocablement à la compétence des tribunaux fédéraux et provinciaux siégeant à Toronto, dans de la province d'Ontario et consent à instituer tout litige qui pourrait découler de la présente auprès des tribunaux situés dans le district judiciaire de York, province d'Ontario.

Au cas où vous auriez des questions concernant cette licence ou que vous désiriez vous mettre en rapport avec Microsoft pour quelque raison que ce soit, veuillez utiliser l'information contenue dans le Contenu Sous Licence pour contacter la filiale de succursale Microsoft desservant votre pays, dont l'adresse est fournie dans ce produit, ou visitez écrivez à : Microsoft sur le World Wide Web à http://www.microsoft.com

Contents

About This Course

This section provides you with a brief description of the course, audience, suggested prerequisites, and course objectives.

Description

The goal of this two-day course is to provide students with the skills and knowledge necessary to configure a Windows-based computer to operate in a Microsoft® Windows® Server 2003 networking infrastructure.

Audience

The target audience for this course includes individuals who are either employed by, or who are seeking employment as, a Systems Administrator in Medium and Large (M/LORG) organizations. The entry criterion for this course includes individuals who are:

- Entry-level IT professionals, new to hands-on Windows server and network administration.
- Preparing for exam 70-291, *Implementing, Managing, and Maintaining a Microsoft Windows Server 2003 Network Infrastructure*, a core requirement for the MCSA and MCSE certification credentials.

Student prerequisites

This course requires that students meet the following prerequisites:

- A+ certification or have equivalent knowledge and skills.
- Network+ certification or have equivalent knowledge and skills.
- Course 2274, *Managing a Microsoft Windows Server 2003 Environment*, or have equivalent knowledge and skills.

Course objectives

After completing this course, the student will be able to:

- Describe the Transmission Control Protocol/Internet Protocol (TCP/IP) protocol architecture.
- Convert Internet Protocol (IP) addresses between decimal and binary.
- Calculate a subnet mask.
- Create subnets using Variable-Length Subnet Mask (VLSM) and Classless Inter-Domain Routing (CIDR).
- Configure a host to use a static IP address.
- Assign IP addresses in a multiple subnet network.
- Describe the IP routing process.
- Configure a host to obtain an IP address automatically.
- Configure a host so that automatic private IP address configuration is disabled.
- Configure a host to use name servers.
- Isolate common connectivity issues.

Student Materials Compact Disc Contents

The Student Materials compact disc contains the following files and folders:

- *Autorun.exe*. When the compact disc is inserted into the CD-ROM drive, or when you double-click the **Autorun.exe** file, this file opens the compact disc and allows you to browse the Student Materials compact disc.

- *Autorun.inf*. When the compact disc is inserted into the compact disc drive, this file opens Autorun.exe.

- *Default.htm*. This file opens the Student Materials Web page. It provides you with resources pertaining to this course, including additional reading, review and lab answers, lab files, multimedia presentations, and course-related Web sites.

- *Readme.txt*. This file explains how to install the software for viewing the Student Materials compact disc and its contents and how to open the Student Materials Web page.

- *2276b_ms.doc*. This file is the Manual Classroom Setup Guide. It contains a description of classroom requirements, classroom setup instructions, and the classroom configuration.

- *Addread*. This folder contains additional reading pertaining to this course.

- *Appendix*. This folder contains appendix files for this course.

- *Flash*. This folder contains the installer for the Macromedia Flash 5.0 browser plug-in.

- *Fonts*. This folder contains fonts that may be required to view the Microsoft Word documents that are included with this course.

- *Jobaids*. This folder contains the job aids pertaining to this course.

- *Labfiles*. This folder contains files that are used in the hands-on labs. These files may be used to prepare the student computers for the hands-on labs.

- *Media*. This folder contains files that are used in multimedia presentations for this course.

- *Mplayer*. This folder contains the setup file to install Microsoft Windows Media® Player.

- *Practices*. This folder contains files that are used in the hands-on practices.

- *Sampcode*. This folder contains sample code that is accessible through the Web pages on the Student Materials compact disc.

- *Webfiles*. This folder contains the files that are required to view the course Web page. To open the Web page, open Windows Explorer, and in the root directory of the compact disc, double-click **Default.htm** or **Autorun.exe**.

- *Wordview*. This folder contains the Word Viewer that is used to view any Word document (.doc) files that are included on the compact disc.

Document Conventions

The following conventions are used in course materials to distinguish elements of the text.

Convention	Use
Bold	Represents commands, command options, and syntax that must be typed exactly as shown. It also indicates commands on menus and buttons, dialog box titles and options, and icon and menu names.
Italic	In syntax statements or descriptive text, indicates argument names or placeholders for variable information. Italic is also used for introducing new terms, for book titles, and for emphasis in the text.
Title Capitals	Indicate domain names, user names, computer names, directory names, and folder and file names, except when specifically referring to case-sensitive names. Unless otherwise indicated, you can use lowercase letters when you type a directory name or file name in a dialog box or at a command prompt.
ALL CAPITALS	Indicate the names of keys, key sequences, and key combinations—for example, ALT+SPACEBAR.
`monospace`	Represents code samples or examples of screen text.
[ ]	In syntax statements, enclose optional items. For example, [*filename*] in command syntax indicates that you can choose to type a file name with the command. Type only the information within the brackets, not the brackets themselves.
{ }	In syntax statements, enclose required items. Type only the information within the braces, not the braces themselves.
|	In syntax statements, separates an either/or choice.
►	Indicates a procedure with sequential steps.
...	In syntax statements, specifies that the preceding item may be repeated.
. . .	Represents an omitted portion of a code sample.

Microsoft®
Training &
Certification

Introduction

Contents

Introduction

- Name
- Company affiliation
- Title/function
- Job responsibility
- Networking experience
- Windows experience
- Expectations for the course

Course Materials

- Name card
- Student workbook
- Student Materials compact disc
- Course evaluation

The following materials are included with your kit:

- *Name card.* Write your name on both sides of the name card.

- *Student workbook.* The student workbook contains the material covered in class, in addition to the hands-on lab exercises.

- *Student Materials compact disc.* The Student Materials compact disc contains the Web page that provides you with links to resources pertaining to this course, including additional readings, review and lab answers, lab files, multimedia presentations, and course-related Web sites.

> **Note** To open the Web page, insert the Student Materials compact disc into the CD-ROM drive, and then in the root directory of the compact disc, double-click **Autorun.exe** or **Default.htm**.

- *Assessments.* There are assessments for each lesson, located on the Student Materials compact disc. You can use them as preassessments to identify areas of difficulty, or you can use them as postassessments to validate learning.

- *Course evaluation.* To provide feedback on the course, training facility, and instructor, you will have the opportunity to complete an online evaluation near the end of the course.

- *Evaluation software.* An evaluation copy of Microsoft® Windows® Server 2003 Release Candidate 2 (RC2) is provided for your personal use only.

To provide additional comments or feedback on the course, send e-mail to support@mscourseware.com. To inquire about the Microsoft Certified Professional program, send e-mail to mcphelp@microsoft.com.

Additional Reading from Microsoft Press

Microsoft Windows Server 2003 books from Microsoft Press® can help you do your job—from the planning and evaluation stages through deployment and ongoing support —with solid technical information to help you get the most out of the Windows Server 2003 key features and enhancements. The following titles supplement the skills taught in this course:

Title	ISBN
Microsoft Windows Server 2003 Admin Pocket Consultant	0-7356-1354-0
Microsoft Windows Server 2003 TCP/IP Protocols and Services Technical Reference	0-7356-1291-9
Microsoft Windows Server 2003 Administrator's Companion	0-7356-1367-2
Microsoft Windows Server 2003 Security Administrator's Companion	0-7356-1574-8
Understanding IPv6	0-7356-1245-5

Prerequisites

- CompTIA A+ certification or equivalent knowledge and skills
- CompTIA Network+ certification or equivalent knowledge and skills
- Completion of Course 2274, *Managing a Microsoft Windows Server 2003 Environment*, or equivalent knowledge and skills

---

This course requires that you meet the following prerequisites:

- CompTIA A+ certification or equivalent knowledge and skills.
- CompTIA Network+ certification or equivalent knowledge and skills.
- Completion of Course 2274, *Managing a Microsoft Windows Server 2003 Environment*, or equivalent knowledge and skills.

Course Outline

- **Module 1: Reviewing the Suite of TCP/IP Protocols**
- **Module 2: Assigning IP Addresses in a Multiple Subnet Network**
- **Module 3: Configuring a Client IP Address**
- **Module 4: Configuring a Client for Name Resolution**
- **Module 5: Isolating Common Connectivity Issues**

Module 1, "Reviewing the Suite of TCP/IP Protocols," reviews the suite of Transmission Control Protocol/Internet Protocols (TCP/IP) protocols. By understanding the function of each of the protocols and how the protocols relate to each other, you have the context for understanding network administration tasks and network troubleshooting.

Module 2, "Assigning IP Addresses in a Multiple Subnet Network," explains how to construct and assign IP addresses and how to isolate addressing issues associated with the IP routing process.

Module 3, "Configuring a Client IP Address," discusses how to configure an Internet Protocol (IP) address for a client computer running Microsoft Windows Server 2003 on a network running the TCP/IP protocol suite. System administrators must be able to configure a client to use a static IP address and configure a client to obtain an IP address automatically.

Module 4, "Configuring a Client for Name Resolution," discusses how Network Basic Input/Output System (NetBIOS) names are resolved into IP addresses. To ensure that clients can communicate on a TCP/IP network, system administrators must know how to configure clients to use the various types of name resolution mechanisms provided by the Windows operating systems.

Module 5, "Isolating Common Connectivity Issues," describes the most common types of connectivity issues and how to isolate them by using a variety of network utilities.

Appendices

Appendix A, "Differences Between the Microsoft Windows 2000 Server Family and the Microsoft Windows Server 2003 Family," explains the differences between the operating systems in the context of the tasks in each module. This appendix is provided for students who are familiar with Windows 2000 Server.

Appendix B, "Decimal Equivalent Mask Values" provides values for IP address classes A, B and C. Refer to these values when completing the practice Calculating a Subnet Mask, in Module 2, "Assigning IP Addresses in a Multiple Subnet Network."

Appendix C, "Problem Isolation Flowchart" describes a problem isolation process. Refer to this flowchart when completing the lab exercises.

Setup

- Classroom is configured as one Windows Server 2003 domain: nwtraders.msft
- London is a domain controller and the instructor computer
- Student computers are running Windows Server 2003 Enterprise Edition RC2
- Each student computer has an organizational unit
- Students are administrators for their server and organizational unit

Course files

There are files associated with the labs and practices in this course. The lab files are located in the C:\MOC\2276 folder on the student computers.

Classroom setup

The classroom configuration consists of two domain controllers and at least 12 student computers. Each computer is running Windows Server 2003, Enterprise Edition.

The name of the domain is nwtraders.msft. It is named after Northwind Traders, a fictitious company that has offices worldwide. The names of the computers correspond with the names of the cities where the fictitious offices are located.

The domain controller is named London. The student computers are named after various cities, such as Acapulco, Bonn, and Casablanca. The name of each computer corresponds with an organizational unit of the same name. For example, the Acapulco computer is part of the Acapulco organizational unit.

Microsoft Official Curriculum

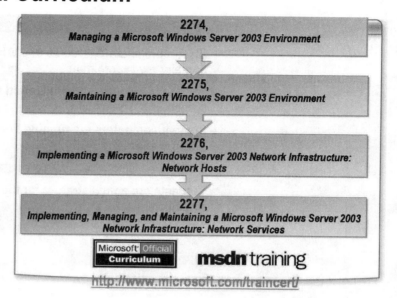

Introduction

Microsoft Training and Certification develops Microsoft Official Curriculum (MOC), including Microsoft MSDN® Training, for computer professionals who design, develop, support, implement, or manage solutions by using Microsoft products and technologies. These courses provide comprehensive skills-based training in instructor-led and online formats.

Additional recommended courses

Each course relates in some way to another course. A related course may be a prerequisite, a follow-up course in a recommended series, or a course that offers additional training.

It is recommended that you take the following courses in this order:

- 2274: *Managing a Microsoft Windows Server 2003 Environment*
- 2275: *Maintaining a Microsoft Windows Server 2003 Environment*
- 2276: *Implementing Microsoft Windows Server 2003 Network Infrastructure: Network Hosts*
- 2277: *Managing and Maintaining a Microsoft Windows Server 2003 Network Infrastructure: Network Services*

Other related courses may become available in the future, so for up-to-date information about recommended courses, visit the Training and Certification Web site.

Microsoft Training and Certification information

For more information, visit the Microsoft Training and Certification Web site at http://www.microsoft.com/traincert/.

Microsoft Certified Professional Program

Exam number and title	Core exam for the following track	Elective exam for the following track
Exam 70-291: *Implementing, Managing, and Maintaining a Microsoft Windows Server 2003 Network Infrastructure*	MCSA	

Microsoft
C E R T I F I E D
Professional

http://www.microsoft.com/traincert/

Introduction

Microsoft Training and Certification offers a variety of certification credentials for developers and IT professionals. The Microsoft Certified Professional program is the leading certification program for validating your experience and skills, keeping you competitive in today's changing business environment.

Related certification exams

This course helps students to prepare for Exam 70-291: *Implementing, Managing, and Maintaining a Microsoft Windows Server 2003 Network Infrastructure.*

Exam 70-291 is the core exam for the Windows Server 2003 Microsoft Certified Systems Administrator (MCSA) certification.

MCP certifications

The Microsoft Certified Professional program includes the following certifications.

- MCSA on Microsoft Windows 2003

  The MCSA certification is designed for professionals who implement, manage, and troubleshoot existing network and system environments based on Microsoft Windows 2003 platforms, including the Windows 2003 Server family. Implementation responsibilities include installing and configuring parts of the systems. Management responsibilities include administering and supporting the systems.

- MCSE on Microsoft Windows 2003

  The Microsoft Certified Systems Engineer (MCSE) credential is the premier certification for professionals who analyze the business requirements and design and implement the infrastructure for business solutions based on the Microsoft Windows 2003 platform and Microsoft server software, including the Windows 2003 Server family. Implementation responsibilities include installing, configuring, and troubleshooting network systems.

- MCAD

  The Microsoft Certified Application Developer (MCAD) for Microsoft .NET credential is appropriate for professionals who use Microsoft technologies to develop and maintain department-level applications, components, Web or desktop clients, or back-end data services or work in teams developing enterprise applications. The credential covers job tasks ranging from developing to deploying and maintaining these solutions.

- MCSD

  The Microsoft Certified Solution Developer (MCSD) credential is the premier certification for professionals who design and develop leading-edge business solutions with Microsoft development tools, technologies, platforms, and the Microsoft Windows DNA architecture. The types of applications MCSDs can develop include desktop applications and multi-user, Web-based, N-tier, and transaction-based applications. The credential covers job tasks ranging from analyzing business requirements to maintaining solutions.

- MCDBA on Microsoft SQL Server™ 2000

  The Microsoft Certified Database Administrator (MCDBA) credential is the premier certification for professionals who implement and administer Microsoft SQL Server databases. The certification is appropriate for individuals who derive physical database designs, develop logical data models, create physical databases, create data services by using Transact-SQL, manage and maintain databases, configure and manage security, monitor and optimize databases, and install and configure SQL Server.

- MCP

  The Microsoft Certified Professional (MCP) credential is for individuals who have the skills to successfully implement a Microsoft product or technology as part of a business solution in an organization. Hands-on experience with the product is necessary to successfully achieve certification.

- MCT

  Microsoft Certified Trainers (MCTs) demonstrate the instructional and technical skills that qualify them to deliver Microsoft Official Curriculum through Microsoft Certified Technical Education Centers (Microsoft CTECs).

Certification requirements

The certification requirements differ for each certification category and are specific to the products and job functions addressed by the certification. To become a Microsoft Certified Professional, you must pass rigorous certification exams that provide a valid and reliable measure of technical proficiency and expertise.

For More Information   See the Microsoft Training and Certification Web site at http://www.microsoft.com/traincert/.

You can also send e-mail to mcphelp@microsoft.com if you have specific certification questions.

Acquiring the skills tested by an MCP exam

MOC and MSDN Training can help you develop the skills that you need to do your job. They also complement the experience that you gain while working with Microsoft products and technologies. However, no one-to-one correlation exists between MOC and MSDN Training courses and MCP exams. Microsoft does not expect or intend for the courses to be the sole preparation method for passing MCP exams. Practical product knowledge and experience is also necessary to pass the MCP exams.

To help prepare for the MCP exams, use the preparation guides that are available for each exam. Each Exam Preparation Guide contains exam-specific information, such as a list of the topics on which you will be tested. These guides are available on the Microsoft Training and Certification Web site at http://www.microsoft.com/traincert/.

Multimedia: Job Roles in Today's Information Systems Environment

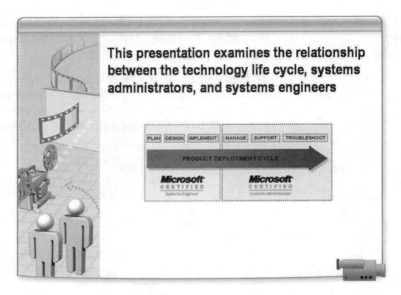

File location   To view the multimedia presentation, *Job Roles in Today's Information Systems Environment*, open the Web page on the Student Materials compact disc, click **Multimedia**, and then click the title of the presentation.

Facilities

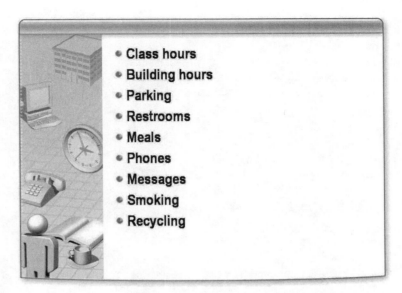

- Class hours
- Building hours
- Parking
- Restrooms
- Meals
- Phones
- Messages
- Smoking
- Recycling

Microsoft®
Training &
Certification

Module 1:
Reviewing the Suite of
TCP/IP Protocols

Contents

Overview

- **Overview of the OSI Model**
- **Overview of the TCP/IP Protocol Suite**
- **Viewing Frames Using Network Monitor**

Introduction

This module provides you with a review of the Open Systems Interconnection (OSI) reference model and the suite of Transmission Control Protocol/ Internet Protocol (TCP/IP) protocols. Understanding the protocols in the TCP/IP suite enables you to determine whether a host on a network running Microsoft® Windows® Server 2003 can communicate with other hosts in the network. Knowing the function of each of the protocols in the TCP/IP suite and how the protocols relate to each other and to the OSI model, provides you with the fundamental knowledge to perform common network administration tasks.

Objectives

After completing this module, you will be able to:

- Describe the basic architecture of the OSI model and the function of each layer.
- Describe the four layers of the TCP/IP protocol suite.
- Describe how the layers of the TCP/IP model relate to the layers of the OSI model.
- Describe the function of each of the TCP/IP protocols.
- Describe how the TCP/IP protocols relate to each other.
- Install Network Monitor.
- Capture and view packets by using Network Monitor.

Lesson: Overview of the OSI Model

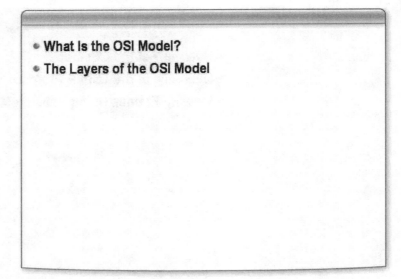

Introduction

To understand how the TCP/IP protocols enable network communications, you must understand the concepts behind network communications. The OSI model is a conceptual model that is commonly used as a reference for understanding network communications.

Lesson objectives

After completing this lesson, you will be able to:

- Describe the architecture of the OSI model.
- Describe how data moves between the layers of the OSI model.
- Describe the function of each layer of the OSI model.

What Is the OSI Model?

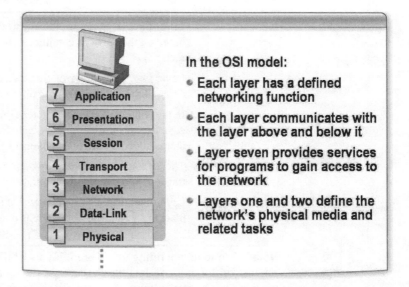

In the OSI model:

- Each layer has a defined networking function
- Each layer communicates with the layer above and below it
- Layer seven provides services for programs to gain access to the network
- Layers one and two define the network's physical media and related tasks

Introduction

The OSI model is an architectural model that represents networking communications. It was introduced in 1978 by the International Standards Organization (ISO) to standardize the levels of services and types of interactions for computers communicating over a network.

Note For more information about the ISO, see International Organization for Standards, http://www.iso.ch.

The Architecture of the OSI model

The OSI model divides network communications into seven layers. Each layer has a defined networking function, as described in the following table.

Layer	Function
Application	Layer seven. Provides an entrance point for programs such as Web browsers and e-mail systems to gain access to network services.
Presentation	Layer six. Translates data between different computing systems on a network. The presentation layer translates the data generated by the application layer from its own syntax to a common transport syntax suitable for transmission over a network. When the data arrives at the receiving computer, the presentation layer on the receiving computer translates the syntax into the computer's own syntax.
Session	Layer five. Enables two applications to create a persistent communication connection.
Transport	Layer four. Ensures that packets are delivered in the order in which they are sent and without loss or duplication.
	In the context of the OSI reference model, a *packet* is an electronic envelope containing information formed from the session layer to the physical layer of the OSI model.

(*continued*)

Layer	Function
Network	Layer three. Determines the physical path of the data to be transmitted based on the network conditions, the priority of service, and other factors.
Data-link	Layer two. Provides error-free transfer of data frames from one computer to another over the physical layer. In the context of the OSI reference model, a *frame* is an electronic envelope of information that includes the packet and other information that is added by the seven layers of the OSI model. The layers above the data-link layer can assume virtually error-free transmission over the network.
Physical	Layer one. Establishes the physical interface and mechanisms for placing a raw stream of data bits onto the wire.

Note   Protocols operating at different layers of the OSI model use different names for the units of data they create. At the data-link layer, the term *frame* is used. At the network layer, the term *datagram* is used. The more generic term *packet* is used to describe the unit of data created at any layer of the OSI model.

Multimedia: The Layers of the OSI Model

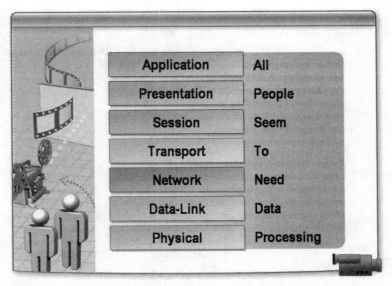

File location

To view the multimedia presentation, *The Layers of the OSI Model*, open the Web page on the Student Materials compact disc, click **Multimedia**, and then click the title of the presentation.

Objective

At the end of this presentation, you will be able to name the OSI layers in order and describe each layer's functionality.

Practice: Putting the Layers of the OSI Model in Order

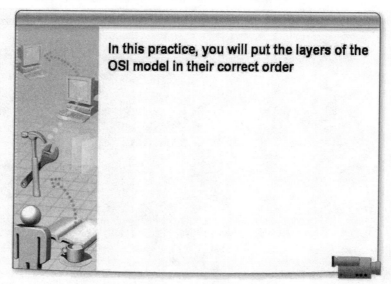

In this practice, you will put the layers of the OSI model in their correct order

Introduction   In this practice, you will put the layers of the OSI model in their correct order.

File location   To perform the interactive multimedia practice, *Putting the Layers of the OSI Model in Order*, open the Web page on the Student Materials compact disc, click **Multimedia**, and then click the title of the practice.

Lesson: Overview of the TCP/IP Protocol Suite

* Why Do I Need to Know About TCP/IP?
* What Is the Architecture of the TCP/IP Protocol Suite?
* How Does the TCP/IP Model Relate to the OSI Model?
* How an IP Packet Moves Through the Suite of TCP/IP Protocols

Introduction

The protocols in the TCP/IP suite enable computers using different hardware and software to communicate over a network. TCP/IP for Windows Server 2003 provides a standard, routable, enterprise networking protocol to enable users to gain access to the World Wide Web and to send and receive e-mail. This lesson describes the four-layer conceptual model of the TCP/IP suite of protocols and how it maps to the OSI model. In addition, the lesson includes a depiction of a packet moving through the TCP/IP layers.

Note For more information about the TCP/IP protocol suite, see Request for Comments (RFC) 1180 under **Additional Reading** on the Student Materials compact disc.

Lesson objectives

After completing this lesson, you will be able to:

- Describe the architecture of the TCP/IP protocol suite.

- Associate the protocols of the TCP/IP suite with those of the OSI model.

- Describe the function of the protocols at each layer of the TCP/IP model.

- Describe how a packet moves through the TCP/IP layers and what happens at each layer.

Multimedia: Why Do I Need to Know About TCP/IP?

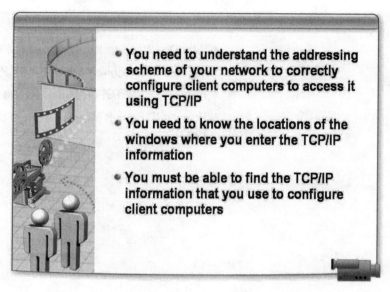

File location

To view the multimedia presentation, *Why Do I Need to Know About TCP/IP?*, open the Web page on the Student Materials compact disc, click **Multimedia**, and then click the title of the presentation.

Objective

After you have completed this presentation, you will be able to explain the importance of understanding client computer addressing schemes and where to configure TCP/IP options on a client computer running a Windows operating system.

What Is the Architecture of the TCP/IP Protocol Suite?

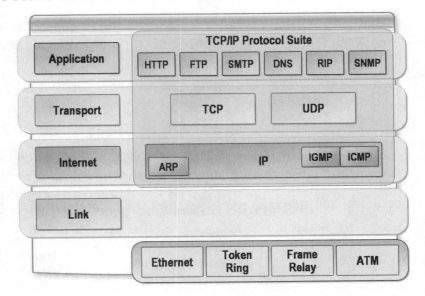

| | **Introduction** | TCP/IP is an industry standard suite of protocols that provide communication in a heterogeneous environment. The tasks involved in using TCP/IP in the communication process are distributed between protocols that are organized into four distinct layers of the TCP/IP stack. |

Introduction

TCP/IP is an industry standard suite of protocols that provide communication in a heterogeneous environment. The tasks involved in using TCP/IP in the communication process are distributed between protocols that are organized into four distinct layers of the TCP/IP stack.

Four layers of the TCP/IP stack

The four layers of the TCP/IP protocol stack are as follows:

- The application layer
- The transport layer
- The Internet layer
- The link layer

Benefits of TCP/IP

Dividing the network functions into a stack of separate protocols, rather than creating a single protocol, provides several benefits:

- Separate protocols make it easier to support a variety of computing platforms. Creating or modifying protocols to support new standards does not require modification of the entire protocol stack.

- Having multiple protocols operating at the same layer makes it possible for applications to select the protocols that provide only the level of service required.

- Because the stack is split into layers, the development of the various protocols can proceed simultaneously, using personnel who are uniquely qualified in the operations of the particular layers.

Note For more information about the TCP/IP application layer and support protocols, see RFC 1123 under **Additional Reading** on the Student Materials compact disc. For more information about the transport, Internet, and link layers, see RFC 1122 under **Additional Reading** on the Student Materials compact disc.

How Does the TCP/IP Model Relate to the OSI Model?

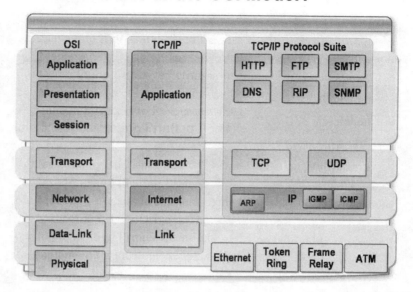

Introduction	The OSI model defines distinct layers related to packaging, sending, and receiving data transmissions in a network. The layered suite of protocols that form the TCP/IP stack carry out these functions.

Application layer

The application layer corresponds to the application, presentation, and session layers of the OSI model. This layer provides services and utilities that enable applications to access network resources. Two services at this layer that provide access to network resources are: Windows Sockets and Network Basic Input/Output Systems (NetBIOS). Both Windows Sockets and NetBIOS provide standard application interfaces for programs to access network services.

Application layer protocols

Some of the applications that operate at this layer connect or communicate with other network hosts are described in the following table.

Protocol	Description
HTTP	Hypertext Transfer Protocol. Specifies the client/server interaction processes between Web browsers and Web servers.
FTP	File Transfer Protocol. Performs file transfers and basic file management tasks on remote computers.
SMTP	Simple Mail Transport Protocol. Carries e-mail messages between servers and from clients to servers.
DNS	Domain Naming System. Resolves Internet host names to IP addresses for network communications.
RIP	Routing Information Protocol. Enables routers to receive information about other routers on a network.
SNMP	Simple Network Management Protocol. Enables you to collect information about network devices such as hubs, routers, and bridges. Each piece of information to be collected about a device is defined in a Management Information Base (MIB).

Transport layer

The transport layer corresponds to the transport layer of the OSI model and is responsible for guaranteed delivery and end-to-end communication using one of two protocols described in the following table.

Protocol	Description
UDP	User Datagram Protocol. Provides connectionless communications and does not guarantee that packets will be delivered. Reliable delivery is the responsibility of the application. Applications use UDP for faster communication with less overhead than using TCP. SNMP uses UDP to send and receive messages on the network. Applications typically transfer small amounts of data at one time using UDP.
TCP	Transmission Control Protocol. Provides connection-oriented reliable communications for applications that typically transfer large amounts of data at one time, or that require an acknowledgment for data received.

Internet layer

The Internet layer corresponds to the network layer of the OSI model. The protocols at this layer encapsulate transport layer data into units called packets, address them, and route them to their destinations.

There are four protocols at the internet layer as described in the following table.

Protocol	Description
IP	Internet protocol. Addresses and routes packets between hosts and networks.
ARP	Address Resolution Protocol. Obtains hardware addresses of hosts located on the same physical network. _Mac address_
IGMP	Internet Group Management Protocol. Manages host membership in IP multicast groups. _Ghost_
ICMP	Internet Control Message Protocol. Sends messages and reports errors regarding the delivery of a packet.

Link layer

The link layer (sometimes referred to as the network layer or data-link layer) corresponds to the data-link and physical layers of the OSI model. This layer specifies the requirements for sending and receiving packets. The layer is responsible for placing data on the physical network and for receiving data from the physical network.

Multimedia: How an IP Packet Moves Through the Suite of TCP/IP Protocols

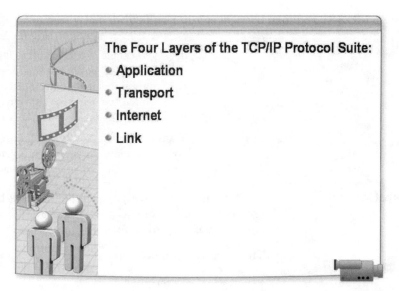

File location

To view the multimedia presentation, *How an IP Packet Moves Through the Suite of TCP/IP Protocols*, open the Web page on the Student Materials compact disc, click **Multimedia**, and then click the title of the presentation.

Objective

After completing the presentation, you will be able to explain the role of each layer in the TCP/IP protocol stack and how an IP packet is sent and received by each layer.

Practice: Associating the Protocols and Layers of the TCP/IP Model

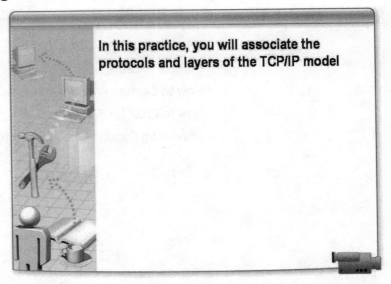

In this practice, you will associate the protocols and layers of the TCP/IP model

Introduction

In this practice, you will associate the protocols and layers of the TCP/IP model.

Practice

▶ **Associate the TCP/IP protocols with the OSI model**

- To perform the multimedia practice, *Associating the Protocols and Layers of the TCP/IP Model*, open the Web page on the Student Materials compact disc, click **Multimedia**, and then click the title of the practice.

Lesson: Viewing Frames Using Network Monitor

- What Is Ping?
- What Is Network Monitor?
- How to Capture Frames
- How to Filter for Select Frames
- Examining Captured Network Traffic

Introduction

Microsoft Network Monitor is a protocol analyzer that you can use to understand and monitor network communications. Network Monitor simplifies your task of isolating complex network problems by performing real-time network traffic analysis and capturing packets for decoding and analysis.

In this lesson, you will use the Ping utility (Ping) to generate traffic for analysis.

Lesson objectives

After completing this lesson, you will be able to:

- Use Ping to test network connectivity.
- Install Network Monitor.
- Capture network traffic.
- Set a filter to highlight specific captured frames.
- Describe the information that is captured by Network Monitor.

What Is Ping?

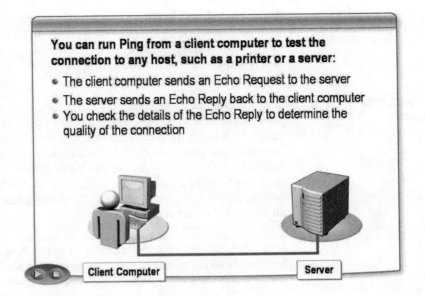

Introduction

TCP/IP implementations include a basic network utility called Ping. You use Ping to test whether a target computer's networking hardware and protocols are functioning correctly, at least up to the network layer of the OSI model. When you use Ping, you generate network traffic. You can then use Network Monitor to analyze this traffic.

Example of using Ping

You run Ping by using the syntax ping *target*, where target is the computer name or IP address of the target computer. In the preceding illustration:

1. The client computer is running the **ping** command specifying the server as the target computer.
2. Ping generates a series of Echo Request messages using ICMP and transmits the Echo Request messages to the server.
3. The server sends Echo Reply messages back to the client computer.
4. When the originating computer receives the Echo Reply messages, it produces an output.

Example of Ping output

When the originating computer receives the Echo Reply messages from the target computer, it produces a display similar to the following:

```
Pinging LONDON (192.168.2.10) with 32 bytes of data: Reply
from 192.168.2.10: bytes=32 time<10ms TTL=128
Reply from 192.168.2.10: bytes=32 time<10ms TTL=128
Reply from 192.168.2.10: bytes=32 time<10ms TTL=128
Reply from 192.168.2.10: bytes=32 time<10ms TTL=128 Ping
statistics for 192.168.2.10:
Packets: Sent = 4, Received = 4, Lost = 0 (0% loss),
Approximate round trip times in milli-seconds:
Minimum = 0ms, Maximum = 0ms, Average = 0ms
```

This display shows the echo replies from the target computer. Information displayed includes the IP address of the target computer, the number of bytes of data included with each request, the elapsed time between the transmission of each request and the receipt of each reply, and the value of the Time to Live (TTL) field in the IP header. In this particular example, the target computer is on the same local area network (LAN), so the time measurement is very short—less than ten milliseconds.

Responses to Ping requests

When you submit a Ping request to, or *ping* a computer on the Internet, the interval is likely to be longer than when you ping a computer on your local network. A reply from the target computer indicates that its networking hardware and protocols are functioning correctly, at least as high as the network layer of the OSI model. Be careful not to assume that simply because a host did not respond to an echo request it is offline or that you are not properly connected to the network. Inability to obtain a reply to an echo request can be an indication of network trouble.

Note   Because of security threats such as the Ping of Death, in which a remote host sends an oversized packet to interrupt service in another system or to prevent outsiders from gaining network configuration information, it is not uncommon for network administrators to prevent external systems from responding to echo requests.

What Is Network Monitor?

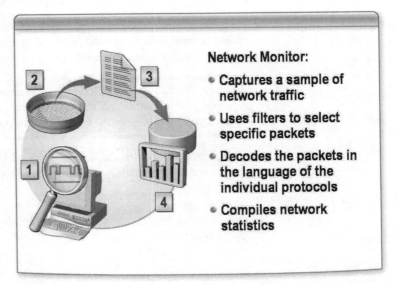

Network Monitor:

- Captures a sample of network traffic
- Uses filters to select specific packets
- Decodes the packets in the language of the individual protocols
- Compiles network statistics

Introduction

Network Monitor is a utility included in Windows Server 2003, in Windows 2000 Server products, and in Microsoft Systems Management Server (SMS).

Uses of Network Monitor

You can use Network Monitor to:

- Locate client-to-server connection problems.
- Identify computers that make a disproportionate number of service requests.
- Capture frames (packets) directly from the network.
- Display and filter captured frames.
- Identify unauthorized users on a network.

How it works

To monitor network traffic, Network Monitor:

1. Captures a snapshot of network traffic.
2. Uses filters to select or highlight specific packets.
3. Decodes the packets in a language of the individual protocols.
4. Compiles network statistics.

Versions of Network Monitor

There are two versions of Network Monitor: one that supports promiscuous mode and the other that supports nonpromiscuous mode:

- In promiscuous mode, the network adapter reads and processes all of the packets transmitted over the physical medium to which it is connected, and not just the packets addressed to it.

> **Caution**   Installing the promiscuous version of Network Monitor may be against your organization's security policy. Obtain appropriate permission before you install the promiscuous version of Network Monitor.

- In nonpromiscuous mode, the network adapter captures only traffic addressed to or transmitted by the computer on which Network Monitor is running.

To run Network Monitor in promiscuous mode, you must have a network adapter capable of switching to that mode. Most, but not all, adapters can run in promiscuous mode.

SMS includes the version of Network Monitor that supports promiscuous mode. To increase security, the version that is included in Windows Server 2003, Windows 2000 Server, and Microsoft Windows NT® Server does not support promiscuous mode.

How to install Network Monitor

You install Network Monitor from the Windows Component Wizard. From **Subcomponents of Management and Monitoring Tools**, select the **Network Monitor Tools** check box, click **OK**, and then click **Next** to continue the installation.

Practice: Installing Network Monitor

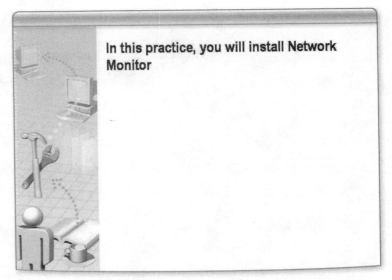

In this practice, you will install Network Monitor

Introduction

In this practice, you will install the promiscuous version of Network Monitor and create a Run as shortcut to run Network Monitor as Administrator while logged on as *Computer*User.

Practice

▶ **Install Network Monitor**

1. Log on to your computer with your *Computer*User account (where *Computer* is the name of your computer) and a password of **P@ssw0rd**.

2. In Control Panel, press SHIFT and right-click **Add or Remove Programs**.

3. Click **Run as**, and then click **The following user**.

4. In the **User name** box, verify that *Computer*\Administrator appears.

5. In the **Password** box, type **P@ssw0rd** and click **OK**.

6. Click **Add/Remove Windows Components**.

7. In the Windows Components Wizard, click **Management and Monitoring Tools**, and then click **Details**.

8. In **Subcomponents of Management and Monitoring Tools**, select the **Network Monitor Tools** check box, and then click **OK**.

9. Click **Next**.

10. If you are prompted for additional files, click **OK**. In the **Copy files from** box, type **\\london\setup\i386** and then click **OK**.

11. Click **Finish**, and then close **Add or Remove Programs**.

How to Capture Frames

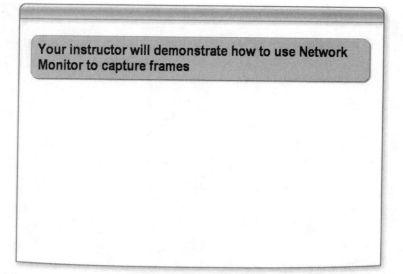

Your instructor will demonstrate how to use Network Monitor to capture frames

Introduction

Network Monitor enables you to capture frames of network traffic for analysis.

Procedure

▶ **To capture frames by using Network Monitor**

1. Open Network Monitor.

2. Select the network interface that you want to use (if it has not already been selected).

3. Start the capture process by clicking **Start Capture** on the toolbar.

4. To stop the capture, on the toolbar, click **Stop and View Capture**. Do not close the capture window.

Network Monitor can also be operated from the command line. For example, if you have already created a filter named http.cf, use the following command to start Network Monitor and use that filter:

```
start netmon /capturefilter d:\captures\http.cf
```

Note For more information about how to use Network Monitor from the command line, see Network Monitor online Help, and "Troubleshooting Performance" in the System Performance Troubleshooting Guide of the *Microsoft Windows Server 2003 Resource Kit*.

Practice: Capturing Frames

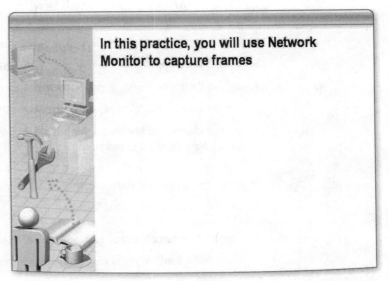

In this practice, you will use Network
Monitor to capture frames

Introduction

In this practice, you will use Run as to open a command prompt and Network
Monitor and then use Network Monitor to capture and display frames.

Scenario

You are the systems administrator for an organizational unit on a network and
are isolating connectivity issues between two hosts. A protocol expert has
requested that you capture ICMP traffic between the two hosts for further
analysis.

Practice

▶ **Start Network Monitor**

1. On the **Start** menu, click **Control Panel** and then double-click
   Administrative Tools.

2. Press SHIFT and right-click **Network Monitor**.

3. Click **Run as**, and then click **The following user**.

4. In the **User name** box, verify that *Computer*\Administrator appears.

5. In the **Password** box, type **P@ssw0rd** and click **OK**.

6. If you are prompted to select a network, click **OK**.

7. In the **Select a Network** dialog box, expand **Local Computer**, click **Local
   Area Connection**, and then click **OK**.

8. Maximize the Microsoft Network Monitor window and the Capture
   window.

▶ **Capture network data**

- On the **Capture** menu, click **Start**.

  This starts the data capture process. Network Monitor allocates buffer space
  for network data and begins capturing frames.

▶ **Generate and view network traffic**

1. On the **Start** menu, point to **All Programs**, point to **Accessories**, and right-click **Command Prompt**.

2. Click **Run as**, and then click **The following user**.

3. In the **User name** box, verify that *Computer*\Administrator appears.

4. In the **Password** box, type **P@ssw0rd** and click **OK**.

5. At the command prompt, type **arp –d *** and press ENTER.

6. At the command prompt, type **ping 192.168.*x*.200** (where *x* is your classroom number), and then press ENTER.

▶ **Stop the network data capture**

1. Switch back to Network Monitor.

2. On the **Capture** menu, click **Stop and View** .

   Network Monitor stops capturing frames and displays them.

3. Leave the Capture window open.

How to Filter for Select Frames

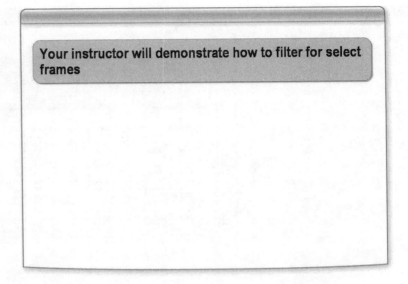

Your instructor will demonstrate how to filter for select frames

Introduction

On a busy network, a packet capture of only a few seconds can consist of thousands of frames, generated by dozens of different systems. You can define capture filters so that only specific frames are saved for analysis. For example, if you want to learn how much network traffic is generated by ARP transactions, you can create a filter that captures only ARP traffic for a specific period of time, and then calculate the number of megabits per hour devoted to ARP from the size of your captured sample.

Procedure

The following steps outline the procedure to filter only ARP packets when capturing network traffic.

1. Open Network Monitor.

2. On the **Capture** menu, click **Filter**.

3. If using the nonpromiscuous version of Network Monitor, click **OK** to close the **Microsoft Network Monitor** dialog box that describes security. Otherwise, proceed to Step 4.

4. Click **SAP/ETYPE=Any SAP** or **Any ETYPE**.

5. Click **Edit**, and then click **Disable All**.

6. In the **Disabled Protocols** list, click **ARP,** and then click **Enable**.

7. Click **OK** to close the **Capture Filter SAPs and ETYPEs** dialog box.

8. Click **OK** to close the **Capture Filter** dialog box.

9. Start, stop, and view the capture.

   The Network Monitor Capture Summary window displays the summary record of all frames.

10. Leave the Capture window open.

Examining Captured Network Traffic

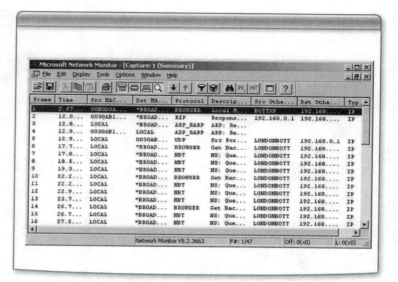

Introduction	When you capture a sample of network traffic, the Network Monitor Capture Summary window displays a chronological list of the frames in your sample. The following table describes the fields that are displayed for each frame in your sample.

Field	Description
Frame	Shows the number of the frame in the sample.
Time	Indicates the time (in seconds) that the frame was captured, measured from the beginning of the sample.
Src MAC Addr	Gives the hardware address of the network interface in the computer that transmitted the frame. For computers that the analyzer recognizes by a friendly name, such as a NetBIOS name, this field contains that name instead of the address. The computer on which the analyzer is running is identified as LOCAL.
Dst MAC Addr	Gives the hardware address of the network interface in the computer that received the frame. Friendly names are substituted if available. By compiling an address book of the computers on your network, you can eventually have captures that use only friendly names.
Protocol	Shows the dominant protocol in the frame. Each frame contains information generated by protocols running at several different layers of the OSI model.
Description	Indicates the function of the frame, using information specific to the protocol referenced in the Protocol field.
Src Other Addr	Specifies another address used to identify the computer that transmitted the frame.
Dst Other Addr	Specifies another address (such as an IP address) used to identify the computer that received the frame.
Type Other Addr	Specifies the type of address used in the **Src Other Addr** and **Dst Other Addr** fields.

Tip To work with large capture files, increase the size of the Windows page file and save large capture files before viewing them.

Practice: Examining Packets

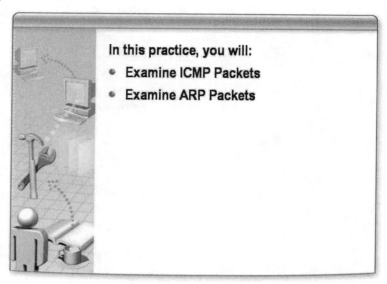

In this practice, you will:
- Examine ICMP Packets
- Examine ARP Packets

Introduction

In this practice, you will change the color of all frames that use ICMP. This is useful when viewing frames for a particular protocol. You will also use Network Monitor to capture and examine ARP packets.

Practice

▶ **Examine ICMP packets**

1. On the **Display** menu, click **Colors**. The **Protocol Colors** dialog box appears.

2. Under **Name**, click **ICMP**.

3. Under **Colors**, set foreground to red, and then click **OK**.

   The Microsoft Network Monitor Capture Summary window appears, displaying ICMP frames in red.

▶ **Examine ARP packets**

1. On the **Window** menu, verify that **Summary**, **Detail**, and **Hex** are selected.

2. On the **Window** menu, verify that **Zoom Pane** is deselected.

   Three separate panes are displayed. The top pane displays the frame summary, the middle pane displays the selected frame details, and the bottom pane displays the selected frame details in hexadecimal notation. As you click in each pane, the window title bar updates with the name of the pane.

3. In the Summary pane, in the Description column, click an ICMP frame that has an entry beginning with **Echo: From** in the description column.

   This frame shows an ICMP echo request from your computer to the instructor computer.

4. In the Detail pane, click **ICMP** with a plus sign (+) preceding it. The plus sign indicates that the information can be expanded by clicking it.

5. Expand **ICMP**.

    The ICMP properties expand to show more detail. The contents of the ICMP packet are highlighted and displayed in hexadecimal notation in the bottom window.

6. In the Detail pane, click **ICMP: Packet Type = Echo**.

    What hexadecimal number corresponds with ICMP: Packet Type = Echo?

    08

7. In the Detail pane, click **Checksum**.

    Record the Checksum number in the table below. *0x9D50*

8. In the Detail pane, click **Identifier**.

    Record the Identifier number in the table below. *512 0x200*

9. In the Detail pane, click **Sequence Number**.

    Record the Sequence Number in the table below.

10. In the Detail pane, click **Data**. The data received in the echo message must be returned in the echo reply message.

11. Repeat steps 1 through 9 for the Echo Reply packet that follows the Echo: From packet that is currently displayed.

12. Close Microsoft Network Monitor and do not save the capture.

Field	Echo	Echo Reply
Packet Type	*08 Echo*	*00 - Echo Reply*
Checksum	*0x9D50*	*0xA55D*
Identifier	*512*	*512*
Sequence Number	*45056*	*45056*

ARP

arp -a   all ip & Mac Addr

Microsoft®
Training &
Certification

Module 2: Assigning IP Addresses in a Multiple Subnet Network

Contents

Overview

- **Assigning IP Addresses**
- **Creating a Subnet**
- **Using IP Routing Tables**
- **Overcoming Limitations of the IP Addressing Scheme**

Introduction

The information in this module describes how to construct and assign an Internet Protocol (IP) address to host computers on a network that is running the suite of Transmission Control Protocol/IP (TCP/IP) protocols. IP addresses enable computers running any operating system on any platform to communicate by providing unique identifiers. To send data between multiple subnets, IP must select a route. Understanding the IP routing procedures will assist you in constructing and assigning the appropriate IP addresses for hosts on your network.

Note In this module, the term *host* refers to any device on the network that has an IP address. The term *client* refers to a computer running a Microsoft® Windows® operating system on a network running TCP/IP.

Objectives

After completing this module, you will be able to:

- Convert IP address from decimal notation to binary format.
- Construct and assign IP addresses.
- Create a subnet.
- Calculate a subnet mask.
- Use an IP routing table.
- Reduce the number of wasted IP addresses.
- Implement supernetting.

Lesson: Assigning IP Addresses

- The Components of an IP Address
- What Are the Classes of IP Addresses?
- How Dotted Decimal Notation Relates to Binary Numbers
- How to Convert Dotted Decimal Notation to Binary Format
- How Subnet Masks Work
- Guidelines for IP Addressing

Introduction

The primary function of IP is to add address information to data packets and route them across the network. To understand how IP accomplishes this, it is necessary for you to be familiar with the concepts that determine the intermediate and final destination addresses of data packets. Understanding how IP uses address information will enable you to ensure that IP routes data to the correct destination.

Lesson objectives

After completing this lesson, you will be able to:

- Describe the components of an IP address.
- Describe the IP address classes.
- Convert dotted decimal notation to binary numbers.
- Describe how subnet masks work.
- Assign an IP address.

Multimedia: The Components of an IP Address

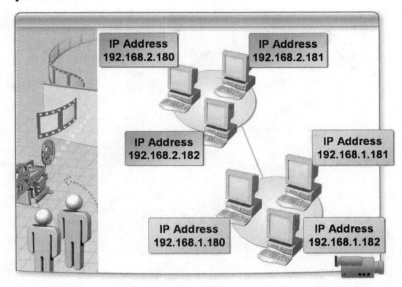

File location

To view the multimedia presentation, *The Components of an IP Address*, open the Web page on the Student Materials compact disc, click **Multimedia**, and then click the title of the presentation.

Objective

Upon completion of this presentation, you will be able to describe how the numbers in an IP address are grouped to designate network and host addresses.

What Are the Classes of IP Addresses?

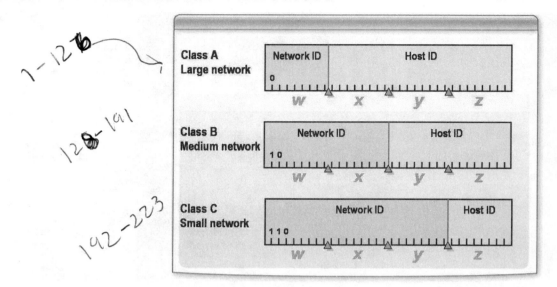

1-12**7**

12**7**-191

192-223

Introduction	IP addresses are organized into classes. You obtain registered addresses through an Internet service provider (ISP) or the Internet Assigned Numbers Authority (IANA). The size and type of the network determines the address class.
IP address classes	The class of address defines which bits are used to identify the network, the network ID, and which bits are used to identify the host computer, the host ID. It also defines the possible number of networks and the number of hosts per network. There are five classes of IP addresses: classes A through E. TCP/IP in Windows Server 2003, and all previous versions of Windows, supports host address assignment for classes A, B, and C.
Network and host ID fields	The four octets that make up an IP address are conventionally represented by w, x, y, and z respectively. The following table shows how the octets are distributed in classes A, B, and C.

Class	IP address	Network ID	Host ID
A	$w.x.y.z$	w	$x.y.z$
B	$w.x.y.z$	$w.x$	$y.z$
C	$w.x.y.z$	$w.x.y$	z

Class A	Class A addresses are assigned to networks with a large number of hosts. Class A allows for 126 networks by using the first octet for the network ID. The first, or high-order bit in this octet, is always set to zero. The next seven bits in the octet complete the network ID. The 24 bits in the remaining octets represent the host ID, allowing for 126 networks and approximately 17 million hosts per network. Class A network number values *for w* begin at 1 and end at 127.

Class B

Class B addresses are assigned to medium-sized to large-sized networks. Class B allows for 16,384 networks by using the first two octets for the network ID. The two high-order bits in the first octet are always set to 1 0. The remaining 6 bits, together with the next octet, complete the network ID. The 16 bits in the third and fourth octet represent the host ID, allowing for approximately 65,000 hosts per network. Class B network number values *for w* begin at 128 and end at 191.

Class C

Class C addresses are used for small local area networks (LANs). Class C allows for approximately 2 million networks by using the first three octets for the network ID. The three high-order bits in a class C address are always set to 1 1 0. The next 21 bits in the first three octets complete the network ID. The 8 bits of the last octet represent the host ID allowing for 254 hosts per network. Class C network number values for *w* begin at 192 and end at 223.

Classes D and E

Classes D and E are not allocated to hosts. Class D addresses are used for multicasting, and Class E addresses are not available for general use: they are reserved for future use.

Using a default subnet mask

When classes are used for IP addresses, every address class has a default subnet mask. When you divide a network into segments, or subnets, you can use the default subnet mask for the class to divide the network IP address. All TCP/IP hosts require a subnet mask, even on a single-segment network. The default subnet mask you will use depends on the address class. All bits that correspond to the network ID are set to 1. The decimal value in each octet is 255. All bits that correspond to the host ID are set to 0.

The following table describes the bit values and number of networks and hosts for the A, B, and C address classes.

Class	First Bits	First Byte Values	Network ID bits	Host ID bits	Number of networks	Number of hosts
A	0	1-127	8	24	126	16,777,214
B	10	128-191	16	16	16,384	65,534
C	110	192-223	24	8	2,097,152	254

Practice: Determining the Class of an IP Address

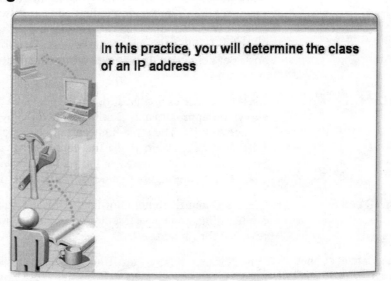

In this practice, you will determine the class of an IP address

Objective

In this practice, you will determine the address class for several IP addresses.

Practice

▶ **Determine the class of each IP Address**

1. Write the address class next to each IP address.

Address	Class
172.16.2.1	B
10.15.7.100	A
192.168.0.100	C
126.0.0.1	A
1.1.1.1.	A

2. Which address class(es) will allow you to have more than 1,000 hosts per network?

    A or B

3. Which address class(es) will allow only 254 hosts per network?

    C

How Dotted Decimal Notation Relates to Binary Numbers

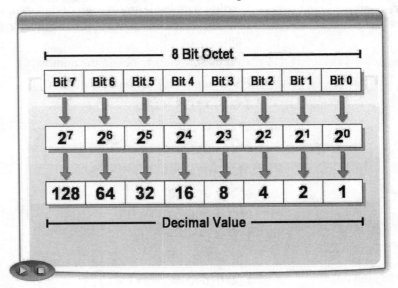

Introduction

When you assign IP addresses, you use dotted decimal notation, which is based on the decimal number system. Computers use a binary format. For you to use dotted decimal notation, you must understand the relationship between these numbering systems.

Computers use a binary number system of base 2 (2 digits, 0 and 1) rather than the decimal system of base 10 (10 digits, 0 to 9). In the IP addressing scheme, computers use the binary format of four 8-bit octets, which yields 32 bits. IP addresses are normally expressed in dotted decimal notation which is four numbers separated by periods, for example, 192.168.0.200. Each of the four numbers represents an octet, ranging from the value 00000000 to 11111111. In decimal notation, the equivalents of these values are 0 to 255.

Each bit position in an octet has an assigned decimal value. A bit that is set to 0 always has a zero value. A bit that is set to 1 can be converted to a decimal value. The low-order bit, the right-most bit in the octet, represents a decimal value of one. The high-order bit represents a decimal value of 128. The highest decimal value of an octet is 255—that is, when all bits are set to 1.

Example of an IP address in binary and dotted decimal formats

The following table shows the binary format and dotted decimal notation of an IP address.

Binary format	Dotted decimal notation
10000011 01101011 00000011 00011000	131.107.3.24

How to calculate the decimal value of a binary number

To calculate the decimal value of a binary representation:

1. Starting with the leftmost digit of the octet, multiply each number in the octet by decreasing powers of 2, beginning with 2^7 and moving from left to right.

2. Add these values to obtain the number.

   For example, for the number 10000011;

   $1*2^7 = 1*128 = 128$

   $0*2^6 = 0*64 = 0$

   $0*2^5 = 0*32 = 0$

   $0*2^4 = 0*16 = 0$

   $0*2^3 = 0*8 = 0$

   $0*2^2 = 0*4 = 0$

   $1*2^1 = 1*2 = 2$

   $1*2^0 = 1*1 = 1$

   $128+0+0+0+0+0+2+1 = 131$

Example of converting from binary to decimal

The following table shows the bit values and the decimal values for all the bits in one octet.

Binary format	Bit values	Decimal value
00000000	0	0
00000001	1	1
00000011	1+2	3
00000111	1+2+4	7
00001111	1+2+4+8	15
00011111	1+2+4+8+16	31
00111111	1+2+4+8+16+32	63
01111111	1+2+4+8+16+32+64	127
11111111	1+2+4+8+16+32+64+128	255

How to Convert Dotted Decimal Notation to Binary Format

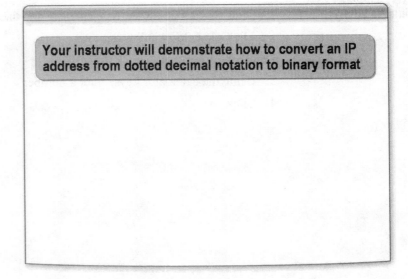

Your instructor will demonstrate how to convert an IP address from dotted decimal notation to binary format

Introduction

Although you can use the calculator in Windows Server 2003 to convert dotted decimal notation to binary format, it helps you to understand the conversion if you can do the calculation manually.

The following table represents the decimal number 131 in binary format 10000011.

Base	2^7	2^6	2^5	2^4	2^3	2^2	2^1	2^0
Decimal	128	64	32	16	8	4	2	1
Binary	1	0	0	0	0	0	1	1
131 =	128	0	0	0	0	0	2	1

Procedure for converting an octet from decimal to binary

To manually convert a number from decimal notation to binary format:

1. Construct a table similar to the preceding one.

2. Determine the largest base 2 number possible in the octet (1 2 4 8 16 32 64 128) which is still less than the decimal number.

3. Place a "1" in the column of that number and zeros to the left.

4. Subtract the base 2 number's decimal equivalent from the decimal number.

5. If there is a remainder, repeat steps 2-4 until no remainder exists.

   The 1s and 0s in your table represent the binary equivalent of your decimal number.

Procedure for using the Windows calculator to convert a number from decimal to binary

To use the Microsoft Windows Calculator to convert a number from decimal to binary:

1. Click **Start**, click **Run**, type **calc.exe** and then click **OK**.

   The Calculator window appears.

2. On the **View** menu, click **Scientific**.

3. Using the calculator keys, enter a number.

4. Click **Bin**.

Practice: Converting Numbers Between Decimal and Binary

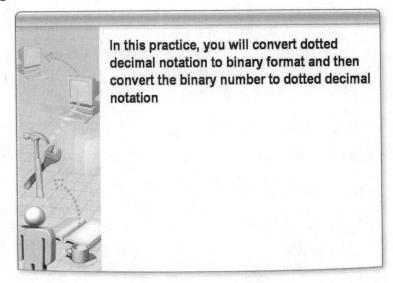

In this practice, you will convert dotted decimal notation to binary format and then convert the binary number to dotted decimal notation

Objective

In this practice, you will convert numbers between decimal and binary.

Scenario

You have been given a set of IP addresses to apply to client computers, and you suspect that one of them has a different network ID. You decide to convert the IP address to its binary equivalent to later determine the correct network ID.

Practice

▶ **Convert the following numbers from decimal to binary**

1. Log on to your computer with your *Computer*User account (where *Computer* is the name of your computer) with a password of **P@ssw0rd**.

2. Click **Start**, point to **All Programs**, click **Accessories**, and then click **Calculator**.

3. On the **View** menu, click **Scientific**.

4. Click **Dec**, type **44** and then click **Bin**.

5. Repeat for each conversion.

Decimal	Binary
44	00101100
97	0110001
255	11111112
192.168.1.100	11000000, 10101000. 00000001, 01100100
255.255.255.248	11111111. 11111111, 11111111.11111000

▶ **Convert the following numbers from binary to decimal**

Binary	Decimal
11111111	63
11111111 11111111 11111111 11111000	255.255.255.248
00001010. 01100100.00000111.00010101	10.100.7.21

Multimedia: How Subnet Masks Work

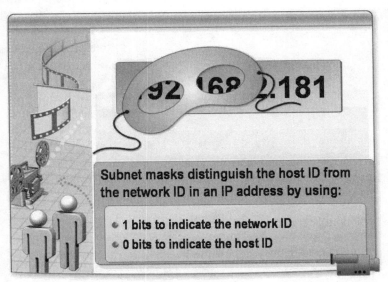

File location

To view the multimedia presentation, *How Subnet Masks Work*, open the Web page on the Student Materials compact disc, click **Multimedia**, and then click the title of the presentation.

Objectives

Upon completion of this presentation, you will be able to describe how subnet masks are used to distinguish the host ID from the network ID in an IP address.

Example of the binary equivalent of a dotted decimal number

A subnet mask's 1 bits indicate the network identifier, and its 0 bits indicate the host identifier. For example, the following is the binary equivalent of 255.255.255.0:

11111111 11111111 00000000 00000000

Practice: Identifying the Components of an IP Address

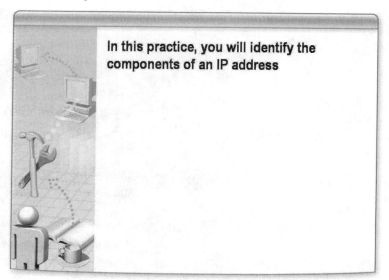

In this practice, you will identify the components of an IP address

Objective

In this practice, you will identify the components of an IP address.

Scenario

You are an administrator and need to identify the network and host ID for a given IP address so that you can determine whether a router is needed to communicate between the two computers.

Practice

▶ **Identify the class of IP address and the default subnet mask**

1. Use the first octet of the IP address to identify the default class and associated subnet mask for the address.

2. Calculate the network ID by using the numeric values in the IP address that correspond to 255 in the subnet mask, and then fill in the remaining portion with zeros (0s).

3. Calculate the host ID by using the numeric values in the IP address that correspond to 0 in the subnet mask.

4. Repeat for each IP address in the following table. The first IP address is completed for you as an example.

IP Address	Subnet Mask	Network ID	Host ID
192.168.0.100	Answer: C/255.255.255.0	Answer: 192.168.0	Answer: 100
10.7.1.1	A/255.0.0.0	10.0.0.0	7.1.1
172.16.1.1	B/255.255.0.0	172.16.0	1.1
129.102.197.23			
199.32.123.54			
1.1.1.1			
221.22.64.7			
93.44.127.235			
23.46.92.184			
152.79.234.1			
200.100.50.25			

nes for IP Addressing

When assigning network and host IDs:

- Do not use 127 for a network ID
- Use public registered addresses only where essential
- Use IANA private address range for private addresses
- Do not use all binary 1's for the host ID in a class-based network
- Do not use all binary 0's for the network ID in a class-based network
- Do not duplicate Host IDs

Introduction

There are no exact rules that govern how to assign IP addresses on your network, however, there are guidelines that you can use to ensure you assign valid network and host identifiers.

Assigning valid network and host identifiers

When you assign IP addresses, consider the following guidelines:

- You must not use 127 for the first octet of the network ID. This value is reserved for diagnostic purposes.

- Use public registered addresses only where essential to do so.

- Use addresses from the private address ranges reserved by the IANA for private IP addressing.

- You must not use all 1s (binary) for the host ID in a class-based network. If all bits are set to 1, the address is interpreted as a broadcast address.

- You must not use all 0s for the host ID in a class-based network. If host bits are set to 0, some TCP/IP implementations interpret this as a broadcast address.

- You must not duplicate host IDs within a network segment.

Private IP Addresses
10.0.0.0 - 10.255.255.255
172.16.0.0 - 172.31.255.255
192.168.0.0 - 192.168.255.255

Practice: Identifying Invalid IP Addresses

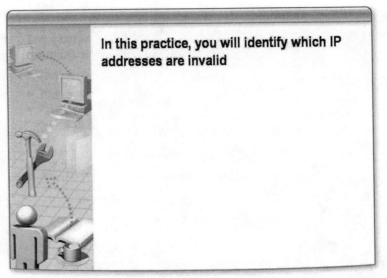

In this practice, you will identify which IP addresses are invalid

Introduction

In this practice, you will identify which of the following IP addresses cannot be assigned to a host and then explain why it is invalid.

Practice

▶ **Determine which of the following IP addresses cannot be assigned to a host**

- Review the following class-based IP addresses. Identify the portion of the IP address that would be invalid if it were assigned to a host, and then explain why it is invalid. Assume a default subnet mask is applied according to the class of the address.

a. 131.107.256.80 _256 only 1 to 255_

b. 222.222.255.222 _OK_

c. 231.200.1.1 _231 > 223 first octet_

d. 126.1.0.0 _as class A OK   as class B Bad_

e. 0.127.4.100 _0 leading_

f. 190.7.2.0 _Sam as d   Bad   for B OK_

g. 127.1.1.1 _127. leading_

h. 198.121.254.255 ____

i. 255.255.255.255 _No broadcast address_

Lesson: Creating a Subnet

- What Is a Subnet?
- How Bits Are Used in a Subnet Mask
- How to Calculate the Subnet Mask
- Defining Subnet IDs

Introduction

You can expand a network by using physical devices, such as routers, to add network segments, or subnets. You can also use routers to divide your network into smaller subnets, thereby increasing the efficiency of the network.

Lesson objectives

After completing this lesson, you will be able to:

- Describe a subnet.
- Describe subnet mask bits.
- Calculate a subnet mask and range of IP addresses.
- Define subnet IDs.

What Is a Subnet?

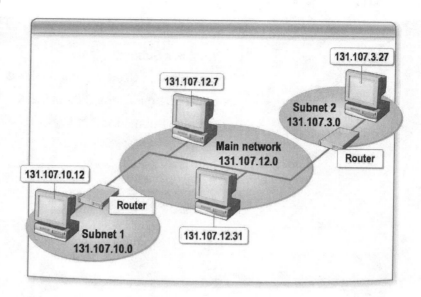

Introduction

A subnet is a physical segment of a network that is separated from the rest of the network by a router or routers. You can have multiple subnets on your network. A network of multiple subnets connected by routers is often referred to as an internetwork. When you create subnets, you must break up the network ID for the hosts on the subnets. Assigning the appropriate subnet and host ID enables you to locate a host on the network. You can also determine which hosts are on the same subnet by matching network IDs.

Subnet IP addresses

The IP address for each subnet is derived from the main network ID. When you divide a network into subnets, you must create a unique ID for each subnet. To create the subnet ID, you partition the bits in the host ID into two parts. You use one part to identify the subnet and the other part to identify the host. The process of creating the subnet ID is called subnetting or subnetworking.

Benefits of using a subnet

Organizations use subnets to apply one network across multiple physical segments. Using subnets allows you to:

- Mix different network technologies, such as Ethernet and Token Ring.

- Overcome limitations of current technologies such as exceeding the maximum number of hosts allowed per segment. Breaking the segment into further segments, increases the total number of hosts allowed.

- Reduce network congestion by segmenting traffic and reducing the number of broadcasts that are sent on each segment.

Considerations for creating a subnet

Before you implement subnetting, you must determine your current requirements and take into consideration future requirements so that you can allow for growth. To create a subnet:

1. Determine the number of physical segments on your network.

2. Determine the number of required host addresses for each physical segment. Each interface on the physical segment requires at least one IP address. Typical TCP/IP hosts have a single interface.

3. Based on your requirements determined in steps 1 and 2, define:

   - One subnet mask for your entire network.

   - A unique subnet ID for each physical segment.

   - A range of host IDs for each subnet.

How Bits Are Used in a Subnet Mask

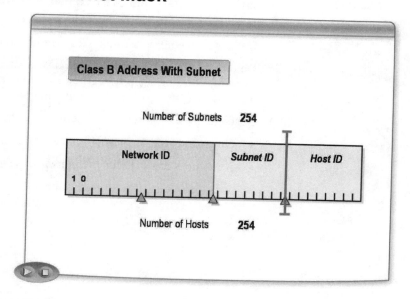

Introduction

Before you define a subnet mask, you must estimate the number of segments and hosts per segment that you are likely to require in the future. This will enable you to use the appropriate number of bits for the subnet mask.

Using bits in the subnet mask

As the preceding illustration shows, when more bits are used for the subnet mask, more subnets are available, but fewer hosts are available per subnet. If you use more bits than needed, it will allow for growth in the number of subnets but will limit the growth in the number of hosts. If you use fewer bits than needed, it will allow for growth in the number of hosts but will limit the growth in the number of subnets.

Contiguous mask bits

When industry standards for subnetting were initially defined, it was recommended that subnet IDs be derived from high-order bits. It is now a requirement that the subnet ID uses contiguous high-order bits of the local address portion of the subnet mask. In support of this, most router vendors do not support the use of low-order or noncontiguous bits in subnet IDs.

Note For more information about subnetting, see Request for Comments (RFC) 950 and 1860 under **Additional Reading** on the Student Materials compact disc.

How to Calculate the Subnet Mask

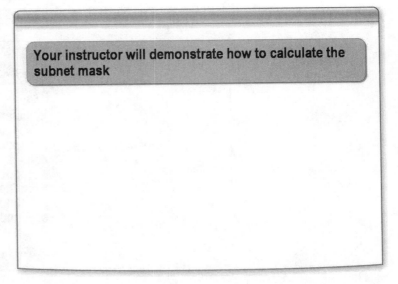

Your instructor will demonstrate how to calculate the subnet mask

Introduction   When you divide your network into subnets, you must define a subnet mask.

Procedure   To define a subnet mask:

1. When you have determined the number of physical segments in your network environment, determine the next-highest power of 2 that is larger than your desired number of subnets. For example, if you need 6 subnets, the next-highest power of 2 from 6 is 8.

2. Determine the exponent required to express this next-highest power of 2. The exponent is the number of bits needed for subnetting. For example, 8 is 2^3. The exponent and the number of bits needed for subnetting is 3.

3. Create the binary bit mask for the octet being subnetted by setting the high-order bits for the number of bits needed to subnet to 1. Then, convert the binary mask value to decimal. For our example, 3 bits are needed. The binary bit mask becomes 11100000. The decimal value for binary 11100000 is 224. The final subnet mask, assuming that we are subnetting a class B network ID, is 255.255.224.0.

Note   For more information about calculating the subnet mask, see Appendix B "Decimal Equivalent Mask Values" on the Student Materials compact disc.

Defining Subnet IDs

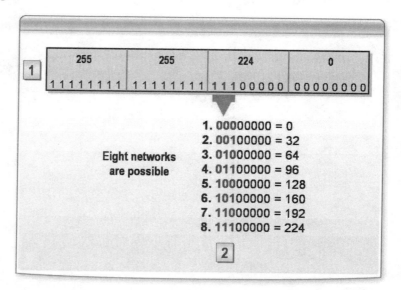

Introduction

To define the subnet ID for a subnet, you use the same number of host bits that are used for the subnet mask. You evaluate the possible bit combinations and then convert them to a decimal format.

How to define a range of subnet IDs

To define a range of subnet IDs for an internetwork:

1. Using the same number of bits as are used for the subnet mask, list all possible bit combinations. In the previous example, 3 bits are required.

2. Convert to decimal the subnet ID bits for each subnet. Each decimal value represents a single subnet. This value is used to define the range of host IDs for a subnet.

Shortcut to defining subnet IDs

Using the previous method is impractical when you are using more than 4 bits for your subnet mask because it requires listing and converting many bit combinations.

To define a range of subnet IDs:

1. List the number of bits in high order used for the subnet ID. For example, if 5 bits are used for the subnet mask, the binary octet is 11111000.

2. Convert the bit with the lowest value to decimal format. This is the increment value to determine each successive subnet ID. For example, if you use 5 bits, the lowest value is 8.

3. Starting with zero, increment the value for each successive subnet until you have enumerated the maximum number of subnets.

How to determine the number of valid subnets

To determine the number of valid subnets, raise 2 to the power of the number of bits being used for subnetting. For example, when you are using 5 bits to subnet, the number of subnets is 2^5, or 32.

Special case subnet addresses

Request for Comment (RFC) 950 originally forbade the use of the subnetted network IDs where the bits being used for subnetting are set to all 0s (the all-zeros subnet) and all 1s (the all-ones subnet). The all-zeros subnet caused problems for early routing protocols and the all-ones subnet conflicts with a special broadcast address called the all-subnets directed broadcast address.

However, RFC 1812 now permits the use of the all-zeros and all-ones subnets in a classless environment. Classless environments use modern routing protocols that do not have a problem with the all-zeros subnet and the all-subnets directed broadcast is no longer relevant.

The all-zeros and all-ones subnets may cause problems for hosts or routers operating in a classful mode. Before you use the all-zeros and all-ones subnets, verify that they are supported by your hosts and routers. All implementations of TCP/IP for Windows support the use of the all-zeros and all-ones subnets.

Note For more information about special-case subnet addresses, see RFC 950 and RFC 1812 under **Additional Reading** on the Student Materials compact disc.

Practice: Calculating a Subnet Mask

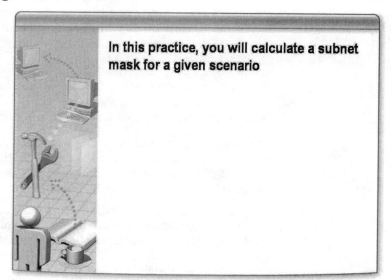

In this practice, you will calculate a subnet mask for a given scenario

Introduction

In this practice, given a number of subnets and an IP address, you will calculate the appropriate subnet mask, subnet IDs, and host IDs.

Scenario

You have been asked to subnet an existing class B network into 14 segments.

Practice

▶ **Determine the appropriate subnet mask**

1. Determine the next highest power of 2 from 14. *1110*

    4

2. Determine exponent for the next-highest power of 2, which is the number of bits required for subnetting.

    16   2⁴   4 bits

3. Convert the required number of bits to decimal format in high order (from left to right).

    255.255.240.0   1111 0000

4. Append the converted number to the existing subnet mask. What is the required subnet mask?

    255.255.240.0

► **Define the subnet IDs**

1. Using the same number of bits as are used for the subnet mask, list all possible bit combinations.

Subnet mask = 255.255.240.0

14

JP0

240.1 — ~~254.~~254 254

0.1 — 15.254
16.1 — 31.254
32.1 — 47.254
48.1 — 63.254
~~64.1~~
64.1 — 79.254
80.1 — 95.254
96.1 — 111.254
112.1   127.254
128.1
144.1
160.1
176.1
192.1
208.1
224.1
240.1

$2^4 = 16$ possible networks

0.0.0	0
0000	16
0001	32
0010	48
0011	64
0100	80
0101	80
0110	96
0111	112
1000	128
1001	144
1010	160
1011	176
1100	192
1101	208
1110	224
1111	240

$2^4 = 16$

4

0000 | 0000
1111

4

2. Convert to decimal the subnet ID bits for each subnet. Each decimal value represents a single subnet. List the subnets and the range of host IDs listed in the following table.

Bit values	Decimal values	Beginning range values	Ending range values
00000000	0		
00010000	16		
00100000	3?		
00110000			
01000000			
01010000			
01100000			
01110000			
10000000			
10010000			
10100000			
10110000			
11000000			
11010000			
11100000			
11110000			

See Previous Page

Lesson: Using IP Routing Tables

- What Is a Router?
- Using a Default Gateway
- The Role of Routing in the Network Infrastructure
- How the Computer Determines Whether an IP Address is a Local or Remote Address
- What Is Static and Dynamic Routing?
- How the IP Protocol Selects a Route
- How IP Uses the Routing Table
- Using the Routing Table in Windows Server 2003

Introduction

In a multiple subnet network, routers pass IP packets from one subnet to another. This process is known as routing and is a primary function of IP. To make routing decisions, IP consults a routing table. To modify and maintain these tables, you must understand how routers use routing tables in an internetwork.

Lesson objectives

After completing this lesson, you will be able to:

- Describe a router and its role in a network.
- Use a default gateway.
- Determine whether an IP address is a local or remote address.
- Describe the difference between static and dynamic routing.
- Describe how the IP protocol selects a route.
- Describe the routing table format.
- Modify a routing table.

What Is a Router?

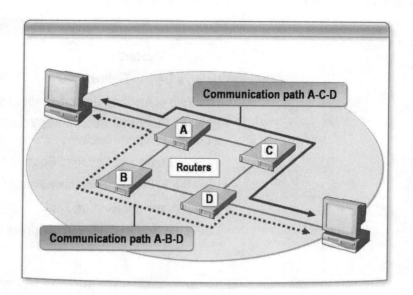

Introduction

In an internetwork, a router connects subnets to each other and connects the internetwork to other networks. Knowing how the router forwards data packets to their destination IP addresses, enables you to ensure that host computers on your network are correctly configured to transmit and receive data.

Routers operate at the network layer of the Open Systems Interconnection (OSI) reference model, so they can connect networks running different data-link layer protocols and different network media.

Example of a router on a small internetwork

On a small internetwork, a router's job can be quite simple. When two LANs are connected by one router, the router simply receives packets from one network and forwards only those destined for the other network.

Example of routers on a large internetwork

On a large internetwork, routers connect several different networks together, and in many cases, networks have more than one router connected to them. This enables packets to take different paths to a given destination. If one router on the network should fail, packets can bypass it and still reach their destinations.

How routers work together

In a complex internetwork, a router must select the most efficient route to a packet's destination. Usually, this is the path that enables a packet to reach the destination with the fewest number of hops (that is, by passing through the smallest number of routers). Routers share information about the networks to which they are attached with other routers in the immediate vicinity. As a result, a composite picture of the internetwork eventually develops. On a large internetwork, such as the Internet, no single router possesses the entire image. Instead, the routers work together by passing each packet from router to router, one hop at a time.

How a router moves packets between networks

Routers use the destination IP addresses in packets and routing tables to forward packets between networks. The routing table may contain all the network addresses and possible paths throughout the network, along with the cost of reaching each network. Routers route packets based on the available paths and their costs.

Using a Default Gateway

When you use a default gateway:

- **The default gateway:**
  - Routes packets to other networks
  - Is used when the internal routing table on the host has no information on the destination subnet
- **DHCP automatically delivers the IP address for the default gateway to the client**
- **To configure the client manually for the default gateway, use the General tab on the Network Connections Properties page**

Introduction

A default gateway is a device, usually a router, on a TCP/IP internetwork that can forward IP packets to other networks. When you configure a client on a subnet and the client requires network access beyond their local network, you must ensure that the default gateway is specified. In most cases, the IP address for the default gateway is automatically delivered by Dynamic Host Control Protocol (DHCP). However, in some cases, you may need to configure the client to use the default gateway.

The role of the default gateway

In an internetwork, any given subnet might have several routers that connect it to other subnets, both local and remote. At least one of the routers is configured as the default gateway for the subnet. When a host on the network uses IP to send a packet to a destination subnet, IP consults the internal routing table to determine the appropriate router for the packet to reach the destination subnet. If the routing table does not contain any routing information about the destination subnet, the packet is forwarded to the default gateway. The host assumes that the default gateway contains the required routing information.

How to configure the client for the default gateway

In most cases, DHCP is used to automatically assign the default gateway. In the event that you need to assign the default gateway manually on clients running Windows Server 2003, Windows 2000, Windows 95, and Windows 98, you configure the property **Default Gateway Address** by using the **General** tab on the **Network Connections Properties** page.

For clients running Windows Server 2003, you can use DHCP to automatically assign the default gateway.

Multimedia: The Role of Routing in the Network Infrastructure

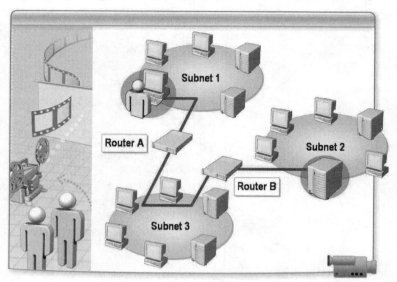

File location

To view the multimedia presentation, *The Role of Routing in the Network Infrastructure*, open the Web page on the Student Materials compact disc, click **Multimedia**, and then click the title of the presentation.

Objective

Upon completion of this presentation, you will be able to describe how IP addresses are used by routers to pass data between networks and subnetworks.

How the Computer Determines Whether an IP Address Is a Local or Remote Address

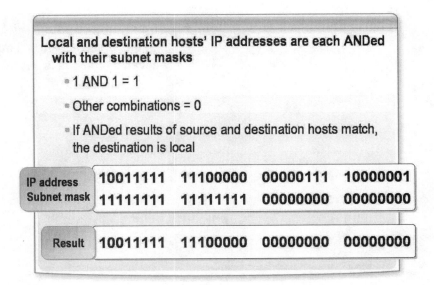

Local and destination hosts' IP addresses are each ANDed with their subnet masks

- 1 AND 1 = 1
- Other combinations = 0
- If ANDed results of source and destination hosts match, the destination is local

IP address	10011111	11100000	00000111	10000001
Subnet mask	11111111	11111111	00000000	00000000

Result	10011111	11100000	00000000	00000000

Introduction

When IP routes a data packet, it must determine whether the destination IP address is on the local network or on a remote network. Understanding how IP makes this determination provides you with the knowledge you will need when you isolate issues associated with IP addressing.

What is ANDing?

ANDing is the internal process that IP uses to determine whether a packet is destined for a host on a local network or a remote network. It is also used to find routes that match the destination address of packets being sent or forwarded.

When IP forwards a packet to its destination, it must first AND the sending host's IP address with its subnet mask. Before the packet is sent, IP ANDs the destination IP address with the same subnet mask. If both results match, IP recognizes that the packet belongs to a host on the local network. If the results do not match, the packet is sent to an IP router.

How IP ANDs the IP address to a subnet mask

To AND the IP address to a subnet mask, IP compares each bit in the IP address to the corresponding bit in the subnet mask. If both bits are 1s, the resulting bit is 1. If there is any other combination, the resulting bit is 0.

Example of bit combinations

For combinations of 1 and 0, the results are:

- 1 AND 1 = 1
- 1 AND 0 = 0
- 0 AND 0 = 0
- 0 AND 1 = 0

Practice: Determining Whether an IP Address Is a Local or Remote Address

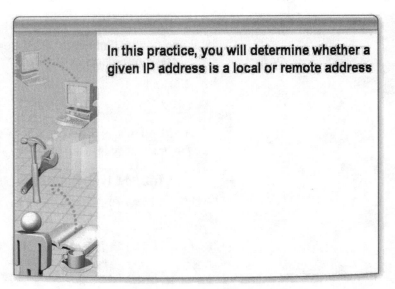

In this practice, you will determine whether a given IP address is a local or remote address

Introduction

In this practice, given your own IP address and subnet mask, you will determine if another address is local or remote.

Scenario

You are isolating connectivity issues between two hosts and need to determine if IP considers these local to each other or remote.

Practice

▶ **Convert both IP addresses to binary and then AND them to determine if they are local to each other or remote**

Your IP address	176.149.115.8
Subnet mask	255.255.252.0
Result	176.149.112.0

Destination IP address	176.149.117.201
Subnet mask	255.255.252.0
Result	176.149.116.0

- Is the destination address local or remote?

  remote

▶ **Convert both IP addresses to binary and then AND them to determine whether they are local to each other or remote**

Your IP address	176.149.115.8
Subnet mask	255.255.252.0
Result	176. 149.112.0

 ~~Remote~~

Destination IP address	176.149.114.66
Subnet mask	255.255.252.0
Result	176.149.112.0

- Is the destination address local or remote?

local

What Is Static and Dynamic Routing?

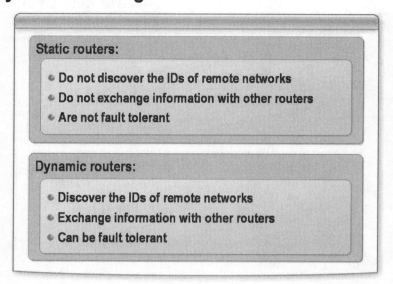

Static routers:

- Do not discover the IDs of remote networks
- Do not exchange information with other routers
- Are not fault tolerant

Dynamic routers:

- Discover the IDs of remote networks
- Exchange information with other routers
- Can be fault tolerant

Introduction

The process that routers use to obtain routing information differs based on whether the router performs static or dynamic IP routing. Understanding each of these routing methods will give you the information you need to maintain routing tables so that IP uses the most efficient route to transmit data to its destination.

Static routing

Static routing uses fixed routing tables. Static routers require you to build and update tables manually. Static routers:

- Do not discover the network IDs of remote networks. You must configure these network IDs manually.

- Do not inform each other of route changes.

- Do not exchange routes with dynamic routers.

- Are not fault tolerant. This means that, when the router goes out of operation, neighboring routers do not sense the fault and so do not inform other routers.

Dynamic routing

Dynamic routing automatically updates the routing tables. Dynamic routing is a function of TCP/IP routing protocols, such as Routing Information Protocol (RIP) and Open Shortest Path First (OSPF). Dynamic routers:

- Can discover the network IDs of remote networks.

- Automatically inform other routers of route changes.

- Use routing protocols to periodically or on demand transmit the contents of their routing tables to the other routers on the network.

- Are fault-tolerant (in a multi-path routing topology). When the router goes out of operation, the fault is detected by neighboring routers, which send the changed routing information to the other routers in the internetwork.

How the IP Protocol Selects a Route

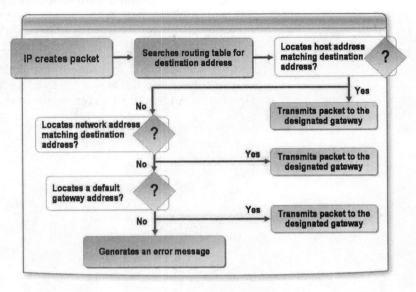

Introduction

To send data packets from one network to another, IP must select the appropriate path. When a router receives a packet, the network interface adapter passes the packet to IP. IP examines the destination address and compares it to a routing table. A routing table is a series of entries, called routes that contain information about the location of the network IDs for the internetwork. IP then makes a decision as to how to forward the packet.

The routing procedure

The IP protocol selects a route by using the following procedure:

1. IP compares the destination IP address for the packet with the routing table entries, looking for a route. A host route in the table has the destination IP address in the Network Address column and the value 255.255.255.255 in the Netmask column.

2. If there is no host route for the destination, the system then scans the routing table's Network Address and Netmask columns for a network route that matches the destination. If there is more than one entry in the routing table that matches the destination, IP uses the entry with the most amount of bits set to 1 in the Netmask column. If there is more than one entry in the routing table that matches the destination with the most amount of bits set to 1 in the Netmask column, IP uses the entry with the lower value in the Metric column.

3. If there are no network routes to the destination, the system searches for a default gateway entry that has a value of 0.0.0.0 in the Network Address and Netmask columns.

4. If there is no default route, the system generates an error message. If the system transmitting the datagram is a router, it discards the packet and sends an Internet Control Message Protocol (ICMP) Destination Unreachable-Host Unreachable message back to the end system that originated the datagram. If the system transmitting the datagram is the source host, the error message gets passed back up to the application that generated the data.

5. When the system locates a viable routing table entry, IP passes the forwarding, or next-hop IP address and interface to the Address Resolution Protocol (ARP) module. ARP consults the ARP cache or performs an ARP exchange to obtain the hardware address of the router.

6. After it has the router's hardware address, ARP passes the packet to the network adapter driver for transmission on the medium. The network adapter constructs a frame using the router's hardware address in its Destination Address field and transmits it on the network medium.

How IP Uses the Routing Table

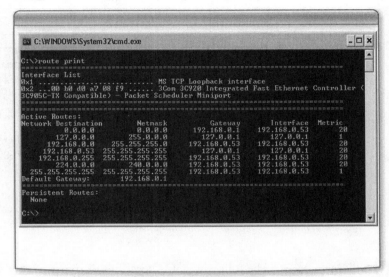

Introduction

To make IP routing decisions, IP consults a routing table that is stored in memory on a host computer or router. Because all IP hosts perform some form of IP routing, routing tables are not exclusive to IP routers.

How the router uses the routing table

The routing table stores information about IP networks and how they can be reached, either directly or indirectly. There are a series of default entries according to the configuration of the host and additional entries that can be entered either manually, by using TCP/IP utilities, or dynamically, through interaction with routers. When an IP packet is to be forwarded, the router uses the routing table to determine:

- The next-hop IP address. For a direct delivery, the forwarding IP address is the destination IP address in the IP packet. For an indirect delivery, the forwarding IP address is the IP address of a router.

- The interface to be used for the forwarding. The interface identifies the physical or logical interface such as a network adapter that is used to forward the packet to either its destination or the next router.

Types of entries in the IP routing table

The following table lists the fields of a route entry and describes the information that they contain.

Route field	Information
Network ID	The network ID or destination corresponding to the route. The ID can be class-based, a subnet, a supernet, or an IP address for a host route. In Windows Server 2003, this is the Network Destination column.
Network mask	The mask used to match a destination IP address to the network ID. In Windows Server 2003, this is the Netmask column.
Next hop	The IP address of the next hop. In the Windows Server 2003 IP routing table, this is the Gateway column.
Interface	An indication of which network interface is used to forward the IP packet.
Metric	A number used to indicate the cost of the route so the best route can be selected. Commonly used to indicate the number of hops to the network ID.

Types of routes

The following table describes the types of routes.

Type of route	Description
Directly attached network ID	A route for network IDs that are directly attached. The next hop field can be blank or contain the IP address of the interface on that network.
Remote network ID	A route for network IDs that are not directly attached but are available across other routers. The next hop field is the IP address of a local router.
Host route	A route to a specific IP address. Host routes allow routing to occur on a per-IP address basis. The network ID is the IP address of the specified host and the network mask is 255.255.255.255.
Default route	A route that is used when a more specific network ID or host route is not found. The network ID is 0.0.0.0 with a network mask of 0.0.0.0.
Persistent routes	A route added with the –p switch. When used with the Add command, this switch adds the route to the routing table and to the Windows Server 2003 registry. The route is automatically added to the routing table each time the TCP/IP protocol is initialized.

The default routing table for a host running Windows Server 2003

The following table shows the default routing table for a Windows Server 2003–based client with a single network adapter, the IP address 192.168.0.53, subnet mask 255.255.255.0, and default gateway of 192.168.0.1.

Network Destination	Netmask	Gateway	Interface	Metric	Purpose
0.0.0.0	0.0.0.0	192.168.0.1	192.168.0.53	20	Default route
127.0.0.0	255.0.0.0	127.0.0.1	127.0.0.1	1	Loopback or testing network
192.168.0.0	255.255.255.0	192.168.0.53	192.168.0.53	20	Directly attached network
192.168.0.53	255.255.255.255	127.0.0.1	127.0.0.1	20	Local host
192.168.0.255	255.255.255.255	192.168.0.53	192.168.0.53	20	Network broadcast
224.0.0.0	240.0.0.0	192.168.0.53	192.168.0.53	20	Multicast
255.255.255.255	255.255.255.255	192.168.0.53	192.168.0.53	1	Limited broadcast

Using the Routing Table in Windows Server 2003

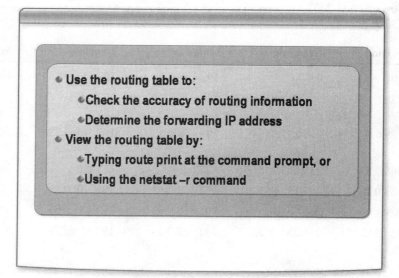

- Use the routing table to:
  - Check the accuracy of routing information
  - Determine the forwarding IP address
- View the routing table by:
  - Typing route print at the command prompt, or
  - Using the netstat –r command

Introduction

You can use the routing tables in Windows Server 2003 to assist you in isolating connectivity issues. Examining the tables will help you to determine if an incorrect entry is contributing to the issue.

How to use the table to identify route errors

If the route for a packet sent out by a host is incorrect, the packet will not arrive at its destination and an error message will be sent to the host. You can examine the routing table to determine the route that was attempted.

To determine the forwarding or next-hop IP address from a route in the routing table:

- If the gateway address is the same as the interface address, the forwarding IP address is set to the destination IP address of the IP packet.

- If the gateway address is not the same as the interface address, the forwarding IP address is set to the gateway address.

Examples of matching routes

When traffic is sent to 192.168.0.55, the most specific matching route is the route for the directly attached network (192.168.0.0, 255.255.255.0). The forwarding IP address is set to the destination IP address (157.60.16.48), and the interface is the network adapter that has been assigned the IP address 157.60.27.90.

When sending traffic to 131.107.1.100, the most specific matching route is the default route (0.0.0.0, 0.0.0.0). The forwarding IP address is set to the gateway address (192.168.0.1), and the interface is the network adapter that has been assigned the IP address 192.168.0.53.

How to view the IP routing table

To view the IP routing table on a computer running Windows Server 2003, type **route print** at the command prompt. You can also use the **netstat –r** command.

Practice: Viewing and Modifying a Routing Table

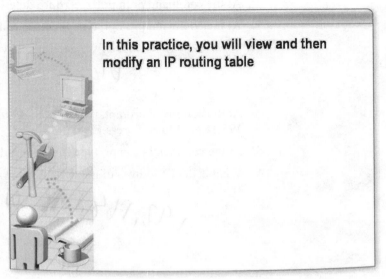

In this practice, you will view and then modify an IP routing table

Introduction

In this practice, you will view and modify the routing table.

Scenario

You have been asked to check a client's routing table for persistent routes and confirm that the IP address of the default gateway is correct. In addition, you must make sure that you can change the default gateway in case it becomes necessary to do so.

Practice

▶ **View the IP routing table**

1. Using Run as, open a command prompt as *Computer*\Administrator (where *Computer* is the name of your computer), type **route print** and press ENTER.

2. Locate the **Persistent Routes** attribute.

3. Are there any persistent routes listed?

   No

4. Locate the **Default Gateway** attribute.

5. What is the IP address of the default gateway?

   192.168.1.200

6. At the command prompt, type **ipconfig /all** and press ENTER.

7. What is the IP address of the default gateway?

   192.168.1.200

▶ **Modify the IP routing table**

1. At the command prompt, type **route delete 0.0.0.0** and press ENTER.

2. At the command prompt, type **ipconfig /all** and press ENTER.

3. What is the IP address of the default gateway?

   its blank

4. At the command prompt, type **route add 0.0.0.0 mask 0.0.0.0 192.168.x.200** and press ENTER.

5. At the command prompt, type **ipconfig /all** and press ENTER.

6. What is the IP address of the default gateway?

   192.168.1.~~x~~ 200

Lesson: Overcoming Limitations of the IP Addressing Scheme

- How IP Addresses Are Wasted
- What Are Private and Public IP Addresses?
- What Is VLSM?
- How to Use VLSM
- What Is Supernetting?
- Using CIDR to Implement Supernetting

Introduction

There are limitations of the IP addressing scheme that can prevent you from using the best scheme for your network, and that result in a large number of addresses that remain unused. In this lesson, you will learn how you can overcome some of these limitations and increase the effectiveness of your IP addressing scheme.

Lesson objectives

After completing this lesson, you will be able to:

- Describe the ways in which IP addresses are wasted.
- Describe the differences between private and public addresses.
- Use Variable Length Subnet Masks (VLSM) to more efficiently assign IP addresses
- Use Classless Inter-Domain Routing (CIDR) to implement supernetting.

Multimedia: How IP Addresses Are Wasted

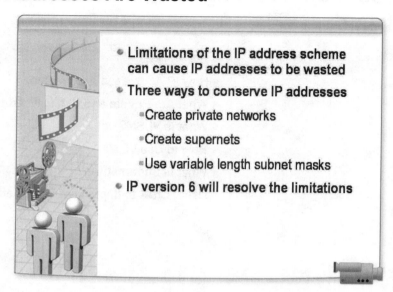

File location

To view the multimedia presentation, *How IP Addresses are Wasted*, open the Web page on the Student Materials compact disc, click **Multimedia**, and then click the title of the presentation.

Objectives

Upon completion of this presentation, you will be able to describe:

- How the limitations of the IP address scheme can cause IP addresses to be wasted.

- Three ways to conserve IP addresses.

What Are Private and Public IP Addresses?

Private addresses:

- Do not have to be registered
- Can be assigned by the network administrator
- Are used on computers that are not accessed by the Internet

Public addresses:

- Are assigned by an ISP
- Consist of unique class-based blocks
- Are kept to a limited number

Introduction

All the computers on your network that are accessible from the Internet require a registered IP address; however, not every computer that can access the Internet requires a registered IP address. You can use private or public IP addresses, depending on network requirements.

Private IP addresses

Private IP addresses are special network addresses that are intended for use on private networks and are not registered to anyone. You can assign these addresses without obtaining them from an ISP or the IANA. You can use private addresses for computers that are not required to be accessible from the Internet.

Note Networks use a firewall or some other security technology to protect their systems from intrusion by outside computers. These firewalls provide computers with access to Internet resources without making them accessible to other systems on the Internet.

A private IP address is never assigned as a public address and never duplicates public addresses.

IP addresses reserved for private networks

The following IP addresses are reserved for private networks:

- 10.0.0.0 through 10.255.255.255
- 172.16.0.0 through 172.31.255.255
- 192.168.0.0 through 192.168.255.255

Note For more information about private IP addresses, see RFC 1918 under **Additional Reading** on the Student Materials compact disc.

How a host with a private IP address sends requests to the Internet

A host that has a private address must send its Internet traffic requests to an Application layer gateway (such as a proxy server) that has a valid public address. Or the host must have a network address translator (NAT) to translate the private address into a valid public address and then send its requests on the Internet.

Public addresses

Public addresses are assigned by IANA and consist of class-based network IDs or blocks of CIDR-based addresses (called CIDR blocks) that are guaranteed to be globally unique on the Internet. There are a limited number of publicly assignable addresses.

When the public addresses are assigned, routes are programmed into the routers of the Internet so that traffic sent to the assigned public addresses can reach those locations. Traffic sent to destination public addresses is transmitted across the Internet.

For example, when an organization is assigned a CIDR block in the form of a network ID and subnet mask, that network ID-subnet mask pair also exists as a route in the routers of the Internet. IP packets destined to an address within the CIDR block are routed to the proper destination.

What Is VLSM?

Using VLSM, you can:

- Create different sized subnets to match the number of hosts in each subnet
- Significantly reduce the number of unused IP addresses

For example:

- If you used a fixed length class C subnet mask (255.255.255.0), you would have allocated 1778 addresses but used only 348, thereby wasting 1430. Using VLSM you can reduce the number of unused addresses to 133.

Introduction	VLSM is a method of creating different-sized subnets in order to conserve IP addresses. When you use fixed subnet mask subnetting on an internetwork that has subnets with different requirements for the maximum number of hosts, a large proportion of the addresses may be wasted. By using VLSM, you can allocate the appropriate number of IP addresses to each subnet rather than use fixed-length subnet masks.
How equal-sized subnets wastes IP addresses	Subnetting was originally used to subdivide a class-based network ID into a series of equal-sized subnets. For example, a 4-bit subnetting of a class B network ID produced 16 equal-sized subnets. In actuality, the number of hosts per subnet is rarely if ever of equal size. This inequality results in many wasted IP addresses.
How VLSM conserves IP addresses	Subnetting does not require equal-sized subnets, so you can conserve IP addresses by using VLSM to create different-sized subnets that best match the number of hosts in each subnet. VLSM is a recursive process that uses subnetting to subnet network IDs that are already subnetted. The process continues until you have unique subnet IDs that waste as few IP addresses per subnet as possible. Because all subnetted network IDs are unique, they can be distinguished from each other by their corresponding subnet mask.

Example of how IP addresses are wasted

In the following table, there are seven subnets that need addresses.

Subnet	Hosts
1	2
2	2
3	62
4	97
5	28
6	153
7	4

If you used a fixed length 24-bit subnet mask (255.255.255.0), you would have allocated 1778 addresses but used only 348, thereby wasting 1430. Using VLSM, you can reduce the number of wasted addresses in this case to 133.

Note Another means of conserving public IP addresses is to use the private address space.

How to Use VLSM

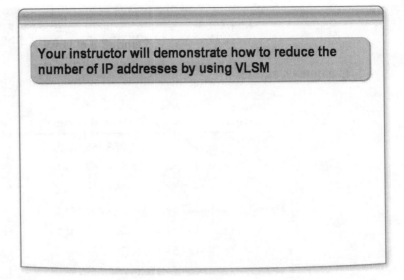

Your instructor will demonstrate how to reduce the number of IP addresses by using VLSM

Introduction

You can reduce the number of IP addresses that remain unused by using VLSM.

For example, given the class-based network ID of 157.54.0.0/16, a required configuration is one subnet with up to 32,000 hosts, 15 subnets with up to 2,000 hosts, and eight subnets with up to 250 hosts.

Note The notation /16 in 157.54.0.0/16 refers to the number of 1 bits used in the subnet mask (255.255.0.0). This is referred to as CIDR notation.

Procedure for one subnet with up to 32,000 hosts

To achieve a requirement of one subnet with approximately 32,000 hosts, subnet 1 bit of the class-based network ID of 157.54.0.0. This produces 2 subnets—157.54.0.0/17 and 157.54.128.0/17. This subnetting allows up to 32,766 hosts per subnet. 157.54.0.0/17 is chosen as the network ID, which fulfills the requirement.

The following table shows one subnet with up to 32,766 hosts per subnet.

Subnet Number	Network ID (Dotted Decimal)	Network ID (Network Prefix)
1	157.54.0.0, 255.255.128.0	157.54.0.0/17

Procedure for 15 subnets with up to 2,000 hosts

To achieve a requirement of 15 subnets with approximately 2,000 hosts, subnet 4 bits of the subnetted network ID of 157.54.128.0/17. This produces 16 subnets (157.54.128.0/21, 157.54.136.0/21 through 157.54.240.0/21, 157.54.248.0/21), allowing up to 2,046 hosts per subnet. The first 15 subnetted network IDs (157.54.128.0/21 through 157.54.240.0/21) are chosen as the network IDs, which fulfills the requirement.

The following table shows 15 subnets with up to 2,046 hosts per subnet.

Subnet Number	Network ID (Dotted Decimal)	Network ID (Network Prefix)
1	157.54.128.0, 255.255.248.0	157.54.128.0/21
2	157.54.136.0, 255.255.248.0	157.54.136.0/21
3	157.54.144.0, 255.255.248.0	157.54.144.0/21
4	157.54.152.0, 255.255.248.0	157.54.152.0/21
5	157.54.160.0, 255.255.248.0	157.54.160.0/21
6	157.54.168.0, 255.255.248.0	157.54.168.0/21
7	157.54.176.0, 255.255.248.0	157.54.176.0/21
8	157.54.184.0, 255.255.248.0	157.54.184.0/21
9	157.54.192.0, 255.255.248.0	157.54.192.0/21
10	157.54.200.0, 255.255.248.0	157.54.200.0/21
11	157.54.208.0, 255.255.248.0	157.54.208.0/21
12	157.54.216.0, 255.255.248.0	157.54.216.0/21
13	157.54.224.0, 255.255.248.0	157.54.224.0/21
14	157.54.232.0, 255.255.248.0	157.54.232.0/21
15	157.54.240.0, 255.255.248.0	157.54.240.0/21

Procedure for eight subnets with up to 250 hosts

To achieve a requirement of 8 subnets with up to 250 hosts, subnet 3 bits of the subnetted network ID of 157.54.248.0/21. This produces 8 subnets (157.54.248.0/24, 157.54.249.0/24 through 157.54.254.0/24, 157.54.255.0/24) and allowing up to 254 hosts per subnet. All eight subnetted network IDs (157.54.248.0/24 through 157.54.255.0/24) are chosen as the network IDs, which fulfills the requirement.

The following table shows 8 subnets with 254 hosts per subnet.

Subnet Number	Network ID (Dotted Decimal)	Network ID (Network Prefix)
1	157.54.248.0, 255.255.255.0	157.54.248.0/24
2	157.54.249.0, 255.255.255.0	157.54.249.0/24
3	157.54.250.0, 255.255.255.0	157.54.250.0/24
4	157.54.251.0, 255.255.255.0	157.54.251.0/24
5	157.54.252.0, 255.255.255.0	157.54.252.0/24
6	157.54.253.0, 255.255.255.0	157.54.253.0/24
7	157.54.254.0, 255.255.255.0	157.54.254.0/24
8	157.54.255.0, 255.255.255.0	157.54.255.0/24

What Is Supernetting?

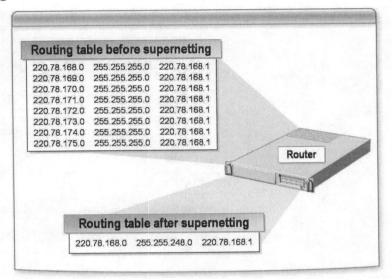

Routing table before supernetting		
220.78.168.0	255.255.255.0	220.78.168.1
220.78.169.0	255.255.255.0	220.78.168.1
220.78.170.0	255.255.255.0	220.78.168.1
220.78.171.0	255.255.255.0	220.78.168.1
220.78.172.0	255.255.255.0	220.78.168.1
220.78.173.0	255.255.255.0	220.78.168.1
220.78.174.0	255.255.255.0	220.78.168.1
220.78.175.0	255.255.255.0	220.78.168.1

Router

Routing table after supernetting		
220.78.168.0	255.255.248.0	220.78.168.1

Introduction

CIDR is a method of assigning and aggregating addresses. One common function of CIDR is supernetting (also known as route aggregation), the process of combining multiple consecutive network IDs of the same IP address class into a single block. For example, you can implement supernetting to collapse multiple network ID entries into a single entry corresponding to the entire class C network IDs allocated to your organization.

How It Works

Supernetting is often used to conserve class B addresses by combining contiguous groups of class C addresses. The class C addresses must have the same high-order bits, and the subnet mask is shortened by borrowing bits from the network ID and assigning them to the host ID portion to create a custom subnet mask.

Example of using supernetting for 2000 hosts

When a company has 2000 hosts on its TCP/IP network that must be accessed from the Internet, it can attempt to obtain the following from IANA or an ISP:

- A single class B network ID. This approach would waste 63,000 addresses.

- Eight different class C addresses that can support 8 x 254 = 2032 hosts. This means poorer routing performance because each router requires eight entries in its routing table for each of the eight networks to which packets can be forwarded.

- A single block of addresses that allows 2,000 hosts. Using supernetting, IANA or an ISP allocates a block of eight contiguous class C network IDs in such a way that they can be expressed as a single routing table entry.

Using CIDR to Implement Supernetting

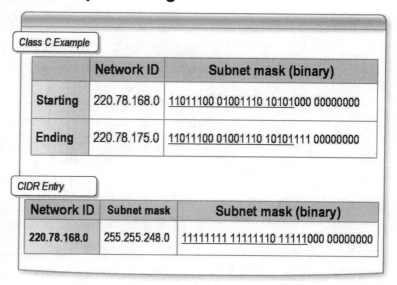

Introduction

When you use CIDR to implement supernetting, you are combining multiple addresses into a single network ID, thereby increasing the efficiency of IP address allocation and reducing the number of unused IP addresses.

How CIDR creates the entry for the routing table

Conceptually, CIDR creates the routing table entry: Starting Network ID count, where Starting Network ID is the first class C network ID and the count is the number of class C network IDs allocated. In practice, a supernetted subnet mask is used to convey the same information.

Example of how CIDR creates the routing table entry

In the following table, eight class C network IDs are allocated starting with network ID 220.78.168.0.

Network ID	Subnet mask	Subnet mask (binary)
Starting Network ID	220.78.168.0	11011100 01001110 10101000 00000000
Ending Network ID	220.78.175.0	11011100 01001110 10101111 00000000

Note that the first 21 bits (underlined) of all the preceding class C network IDs are the same. The last three bits of the third octet vary from 000 to 111. The following table describes the values of the CIDR entry in the routing tables of the Internet routers.

Network ID	Subnet mask	Subnet mask (binary)
220.78.168.0	255.255.248.0	11111111 11111111 11111000 00000000

In network prefix or CIDR notation, the CIDR entry is 220.78.168.0/21. The number 21 refers to the number of 1 bits used in the subnet mask.

Note Because subnet masks are used to express the count, class-based network IDs must be allocated in groups corresponding to powers of 2.

Address Space Perspective

The use of CIDR to allocate addresses promotes a new perspective on IP network IDs. The CIDR block [220.78.168.0, 255.255.248.0] can be thought of in two ways:

- A block of eight class C network IDs.
- An address space in which 21 bits are fixed and 11 bits are assignable.

In the latter perspective, IP network IDs lose their class-based heritage and become separate IP address spaces, subsets of the original IP address space defined by the 32-bit IP address. This is the current and correct perspective as the original Internet address classes have been made obsolete by CIDR.

Each IP network ID (class-based, subnetted, or CIDR block) is an address space in which certain bits are fixed (the network ID bits) and certain bits are variable (the host bits). The host bits are assignable as host IDs or, by using subnetting techniques, can be used in whatever manner best suits the needs of the organization.

Requirements for using CIDR

For routers to support CIDR, they must be able to exchange routing information in the form of Network ID-Network Mask pairs. RIP for IP version 2, OSPF, and Border Gateway Protocol version 4 (BGPv4) are routing protocols that support CIDR. RIP for IP version 1 does not support CIDR.

Microsoft®
Training &
Certification

Module 3: Configuring a Client IP Address

Contents

Overview

- Configuring a Client to Use a Static IP Address
- Configuring a Client to Obtain an IP Address Automatically
- Using Alternate Configuration

Introduction

The information in this module describes how to configure an Internet Protocol (IP) address for a client computer running Microsoft® Windows® Server 2003. An IP address is required for each computer and device on a network that is running the suite of Transmission Control Protocol/IP (TCP/IP) protocols. The IP address identifies a computer's location on the network. When you assign an IP address to a client, you are ensuring that the client can be accurately identified on the network when it sends and receives data.

Note In this module, the term *client* refers to a computer running a Windows operating system on a network running TCP/IP. The term *host* includes clients and refers to any device on the network that has an IP address.

Objectives

After completing this module, you will be able to:

- Configure a client to use a static IP address.
- Configure a client to obtain an IP address automatically by using Dynamic Host Configuration Protocol (DHCP).
- Configure a client to obtain an IP address automatically by using Alternate Configuration.

Lesson: Configuring a Client to Use a Static IP Address

- Static and Dynamic IP Addresses
- How to Manually Assign an IP Address
- Viewing Static TCP/IP Configuration
- Viewing TCP/IP Configuration Using Ipconfig

Introduction

Assigning an IP address is a fundamental procedure for you to establish client network connectivity. By default, Windows Server 2003 is configured to obtain an IP address automatically by using DHCP. However, there will be instances where it is necessary for you to manually assign and confirm the assignment of an IP address. An IP address that is manually assigned is referred to as a static address.

Lesson objectives

After completing this lesson, you will be able to:

- Describe a static IP address.
- Describe a dynamic IP address.
- Manually assign a static IP address.
- View static TCP/IP configuration.
- View TCP/IP configuration using Ipconfig.

Static and Dynamic IP Addresses

> **IP addresses can be:**
>
> - **Static**
>   Addresses that are manually assigned and do not change over time
>
> - **Dynamic**
>   Addresses that are automatically assigned for a specific length of time and may change

Introduction

You can assign either static or dynamic IP addresses for client computers depending on your network configuration and on the computer's function.

What is a static IP address?

A static IP address is an address that always remains the same and must be manually configured. When you assign static IP addresses, you must manually configure the address for each computer on your network.

When to use a static IP address

You use a static IP address when:

- A client or server is using an application that requires an IP address that does not change.

- You do not have a DHCP server on your network.

- You are isolating network connectivity issues for a client computer, and want to determine if a DHCP server is incorrectly configured.

Caution Although manually assigned addresses may provide some benefit, there is the potential for manually assigning duplicate addresses. Assigning the same IP address to more than one client will result in loss of network connectivity.

What is a dynamic IP address?

A dynamic address is an address that changes over time and is automatically assigned. You use DHCP to assign dynamic addresses. When you assign IP addresses automatically, you can configure the addresses for an entire network from a single location and then dynamically assign them to each computer.

Managing IP addresses

Every host on your TCP/IP network must have a unique IP address. This requirement complicates the process of configuring the TCP/IP client. You must be sure that every computer is configured correctly, which means that you must keep track of the IP address assignments. On a small network, configuring the individual TCP/IP hosts, and keeping track of their IP addresses, is relatively straightforward, whether you use static or dynamic addresses. However, on a large network, managing IP addresses can be challenging, and in this case, you can use DHCP to simplify the task.

How to Manually Assign a Static IP Address

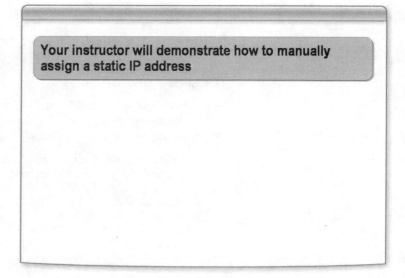

Your instructor will demonstrate how to manually assign a static IP address

Introduction

When you assign a static IP address to a client on your network, you must configure the address manually. To assign a static IP address you use the **Internet Protocol (TCP/IP) Properties** dialog box in Windows Server 2003. To perform this procedure, you must be a member of the Administrators group or the Network Configuration Operators group on the local computer.

Procedure

To open the **Internet Protocol (TCP/IP) Properties** dialog box:

1. From the **Start** menu, point to **Control Panel**, point to **Network Connections**, and then click **Local Area Connection**.

2. In the Local Area Connection Status window, click **Properties**.

3. In the **Local Area Connection Properties** dialog box, click **Internet Protocol (TCP/IP)**, and then click **Properties** to display the **Internet Protocol (TCP/IP) Properties** dialog box. In this dialog box, click **Use the following IP address** to enter values for the IP address, subnet mask, and default gateway. At a minimum, the IP address and subnet mask are required for configuration of a client.

Note In general, most computers have only one network adapter installed and therefore require only a single IP address. When a device, such as a router, has multiple network adapters installed, each enabled adapter needs its own IP address. In some instances, a client may have multiple network adapters.

Viewing Static TCP/IP Configuration

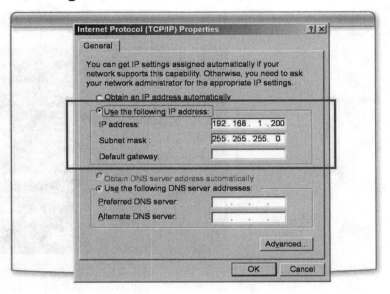

Introduction

In some situations, you may need to view the IP address information for a specific client. For example, a client on your network may not be able to communicate with other computers on the network. In this situation, you must know the IP addresses of the other computers in order to identify the problem.

How to view a static IP address

You can use the **Internet Protocol (TCP/IP) Properties** dialog box to view static TCP/IP information.

Using the **Internet Protocol (TCP/IP) Properties** dialog box, you can determine whether the IP address configuration has been performed dynamically or statically. However, if the IP address has been configured dynamically using DHCP or Automatic Private IP Addressing (APIPA), you cannot determine the values of the TCP/IP configuration options by using this property page. These options include the IP address, subnet mask, and default gateway. You can determine these values by using this property page only if the configuration has been done manually.

You can also use the **Support** tab from the **Local Area Connection Status** dialog box to view IP address information. If the interface has a static configuration, the **Address Type** will indicate **Manually Configured**.

Viewing TCP/IP Configuration Using Ipconfig

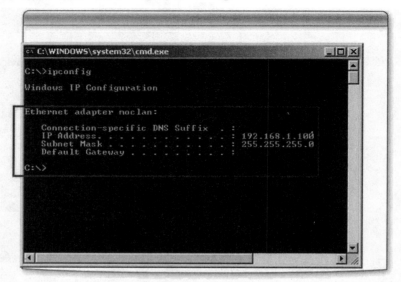

Introduction	When you want to obtain information about dynamic IP addresses, you can use Ipconfig. You can also use Ipconfig to view information about static IP addresses not provided when you use the **Internet Protocol (TCP/IP) Properties** dialog box.
What is Ipconfig	Ipconfig is a command-line utility in Windows Server 2003. You can use this utility to view but not set, the TCP/IP configuration options on a client, including the IP address, subnet mask, and default gateway. The **Internet Protocol (TCP/IP) Properties** dialog box merely displays the specified IP address. Ipconfig provides information such as media state (connected or disconnected).
How to use Ipconfig to view IP addresses	The command syntax for this utility is **ipconfig.** To start the Ipconfig utility, type **ipconfig** at the command prompt. The values of the three primary configuration parameters are displayed.
	If you use the **Support** tab from the **Local Area Connection Status** dialog box to view the IP address, the **Address Type** will indicate **Assigned by DHCP** if the client has a dynamic TCP/IP configuration.

Practice: Manually Assigning and Viewing an IP Address

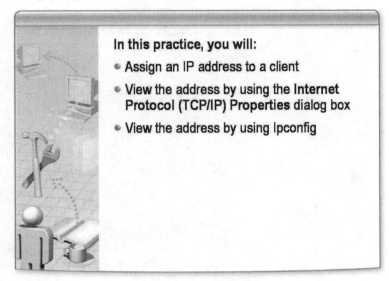

In this practice, you will:

* Assign an IP address to a client
* View the address by using the Internet Protocol (TCP/IP) Properties dialog box
* View the address by using Ipconfig

Introduction

In this practice, you will configure a client to use a static IP address and use the Ipconfig utility to confirm the address assignment.

Scenario

You are part of a client deployment team that is configuring network connection settings. Although most of the clients will require dynamic IP address configurations, a small number of the clients that you are configuring require static IP addresses. Your responsibility is to assign the addresses and verify configuration by using Ipconfig.

Practice

▶ **Assign a static IP address**

1. Log on as *Computer*\Administrator with a password of **P@ssw0rd** (where *Computer* is the name of your computer).

2. Click **Start**, point to **Control Panel**, point to **Network Connections**, and then click **Local Area Connection**.

   The **Local Area Connection Status** dialog box appears.

3. Click **Properties**.

   The **Local Area Connection Properties** dialog box appears.

4. Click **Internet Protocol (TCP/IP)**, and then click **Properties**.

   The **Internet Protocol (TCP/IP) Properties** dialog box appears.

5. Click **Use the following IP address**.

6. In the **IP address** box, type the IP address that corresponds to your computer name in the table below (where *x* is the network number indicated by your instructor).

Computer Name	IP Address
Vancouver	192.168.*x*.11
Denver	192.168.*x*.12
Perth	192.168.*x*.13
Brisbane	192.168.*x*.14
Lisbon	192.168.*x*.15
Bonn	192.168.*x*.16
Lima	192.168.*x*.17
Santiago	192.168.*x*.18
Bangalore	192.168.*x*.19
Singapore	192.168.*x*.20
Casablanca	192.168.*x*.21
Tunis	192.168.*x*.22
Acapulco	192.168.*x*.23
Miami	192.168.*x*.24
Auckland	192.168.*x*.25
Suva	192.168.*x*.26
Stockholm	192.168.*x*.27
Moscow	192.168.*x*.28
Caracas	192.168.*x*.29
Montevideo	192.168.*x*.30
Manila	192.168.*x*.31
Tokyo	192.168.*x*.32
Khartoum	192.168.*x*.33
Nairobi	192.168.*x*.34

7. Press TAB and verify that the subnet mask box displays **255.255.255.0**

8. To close the **Internet Protocol (TCP/IP) Properties** dialog box, click **OK**.

9. In the **Microsoft TCP/IP** message box, click **OK**.

10. To close the **Local Area Connection Properties** dialog box, click **Close**.

11. To close the **Local Area Connection Status** dialog box, click **Close**.

12. At the command prompt, type **ipconfig** and press ENTER.

13. Verify that the IP Address attribute matches what you entered in Step 5.

14. Verify that the Subnet Mask attribute is **255.255.255.0**.

Lesson: Configuring a Client to Obtain an IP Address Automatically

- What Is DCHP?
- Obtaining an Address Using DHCP
- Viewing DHCP Assigned Settings on the Client
- Renewing an IP Address
- Manually Releasing, Renewing, and Verifying an IP Address

Introduction

Windows Server 2003 includes DHCP, a TCP/IP standard that you can use to automatically assign dynamic IP addresses and other TCP/IP configuration parameters to client computers on your network. When you use DHCP, you centralize the management of IP addresses and other TCP/IP configuration settings, thereby simplifying your administrative tasks.

Lesson objectives

After completing this lesson, you will be able to:

- Describe DHCP.
- Configure a client to use DHCP.
- Manually release and renew and verify an IP address.

What Is DHCP?

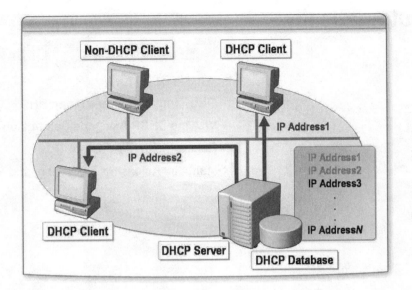

Introduction

By default, Windows Server 2003 is configured to obtain an IP address automatically by using DHCP. The DHCP Server service in Windows Server 2003 is integrated with the Active Directory® directory service and Domain Name System (DNS) service.

What is DHCP?

DHCP is a service and a protocol that work together to automatically assign IP addresses and other configuration settings to the computers on a network. DHCP dynamically assigns IP addresses to clients from a pool of addresses.

Benefits of using DHCP

When you use DHCP, you:

- Do not have to manually configure each client with an IP address.
- No longer have to maintain a record of each individual IP addresses that you have assigned.
- Can automatically assign a new IP address when you move a client from one subnet to another.
- Can release the IP address of a computer that is offline for a specific amount of time, and then reassign the address to another computer.
- Reduce the possibility of address duplication because DHCP automatically tracks IP address assignments.
- Can rely on the DHCP server to detect unauthorized DHCP servers on the network.

How DHCP works

When a DHCP server receives a request from a DHCP client, it selects an IP address from a pool of addresses (called a scope) defined in its database and offers it to the DHCP client. If the client accepts the offer, the IP addressing information is leased to the client for a specified period of time. As the lease interval progresses, the client renews the address assignment each time it logs on to the network. If the lease expires without a renewal, the IP address is returned to the pool for reassignment. Certain addresses in the scope may be excluded from distribution because they are already assigned as static addresses.

The DHCP server provides the client with the following basic information:

- IP address
- Subnet mask
- Default gateway

Other information can be distributed by using DHCP as well, such as DNS server addresses and Windows Internet Name Service (WINS) server addresses.

How to enable DHCP

You must enable clients in the network to use DHCP by clicking **Obtain an IP address automatically** in the **Internet Protocol (TCP/IP) Properties** dialog box, which is selected by default in Windows Server 2003.

Note For more information about DHCP, see Request for Comments (RFC) 2131 under **Additional Reading** on the Student Materials compact disc, and Course 2277B, *Implementing, Managing, and Maintaining a Microsoft Windows Server 2003 Network Infrastructure: Network Services*.

Multimedia: The Role of DHCP in the Network Infrastructure

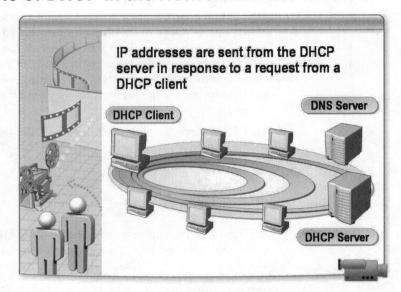

File location

To view the multimedia presentation, *The Role of DHCP in the Network Infrastructure*, open the Web page on the Student Materials compact disc, click **Multimedia**, and then click the title of the presentation.

Objectives

At the end of this presentation, you will be able to describe how DHCP:

- Assigns TCP/IP configuration data to clients.
- Manages IP address allocation.
- Ensures IP address conflicts do not occur.
- Provides configuration data for a specific period of time.

Viewing DHCP Assigned Settings on the Client

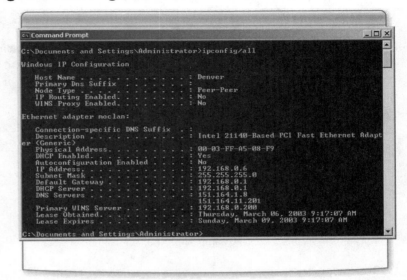

Introduction

When you want to confirm that information configured on the DHCP server has been successfully distributed to a client, you can use the Ipconfig utility that is included in Windows Server 2003. By using this utility, you can view the parameters assigned by DHCP and thereby ensure that IP addresses for client computers are configured correctly.

How to obtain DHCP information by using Ipconfig

You can obtain more detailed information about how a client is using DHCP by using the Ipconfig utility and specifying the **/all** switch. To use the Ipconfig utility with this switch, type **ipconfig /all** at the command prompt. The screen displays the information about all TCP/IP configuration options. You can now determine whether DHCP is enabled. If the value of the **DHCP Enabled** attribute is **Yes**, and a DHCP server IP address is displayed, then the IP address has been obtained by using DHCP.

A DHCP server leases an IP address to a client for a specific length of time. The **Lease Obtained** and **Lease Expires** attributes display information on when the lease was obtained and when it will expire. If a DHCP server is unavailable to assign an IP address and the IP address is assigned automatically, the word autoconfiguration precedes the value for the IP address of the computer. In this case, the **Autoconfiguration Enabled** value would be **Yes**. The DHCP server IP address attribute would not be displayed.

Practice: Configuring a Client to Use DHCP

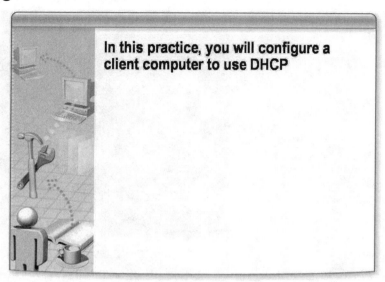

In this practice, you will configure a client computer to use DHCP

Introduction

In this practice, you will configure a client to use a dynamic IP address.

Scenario

You are part of a client deployment team that is configuring network connection settings. Your team is responsible for implementing a change from a static addressing scheme to using DHCP. One of the clients has been configured to use a static IP address and you must change it to obtain an address by using DHCP.

Practice

▶ **Configure a client to use DHCP**

1. Click **Start**, point to **Control Panel**, point to **Network Connections**, and then click **Local Area Connection**.

   The **Local Area Connection Status** dialog box appears.

2. Click **Properties**.

   The **Local Area Connection Properties** dialog box appears.

3. Click **Internet Protocol (TCP/IP)**, and then click **Properties**.

   The **Internet Protocol (TCP/IP) Properties** dialog box appears.

4. Click **Obtain an IP address automatically**.

5. Click **Obtain DNS server address automatically**, and then click **OK**.

6. To close the **Local Area Connection Properties** dialog box, click **Close**.

7. To close the **Local Area Connection Status** dialog box, click **Close**.

8. Open a command prompt, type **ipconfig /all** and press ENTER.

9. Locate the line in the output that reads **DHCP Enabled**.

   Is the IP address dynamic or static?

   Dynamic

10. Close all windows and log off.

Renewing an IP Address

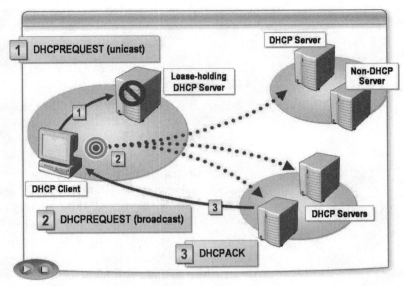

Introduction

When you identify a connectivity issue with a client on your network, often an effective first step is to manually release and renew the IP address. This action frequently resolves the issue. For example, when you move a client from one subnet to another, the IP address may not be automatically updated for the new subnet. In this case, releasing and renewing the IP address may be all you need to do to solve the problem.

Automatic renewal of IP addresses

In most cases, the client retains the settings assigned to it by the DHCP server until someone explicitly changes them or forces a reassignment. However, when the server dynamically allocates settings, the client leases its IP address for a certain period of time (configured at the server) and must renew the lease to continue using it.

The length of an IP address lease is typically measured in days, and is generally based on whether computers are frequently moved around the network or whether IP addresses are in short supply. Shorter leases generate more network traffic, but enable DHCP servers to reclaim unused addresses faster. For a relatively stable network, longer leases reduce the amount of traffic that DHCP generates.

The lease renewal process

The lease renewal process begins when a *bound client* (a DHCP client with a leased address) reaches what is known as the *renewal time value,* or *T1 value,* of its lease. By default, the renewal time value is 50 percent of the lease period. When a client reaches this point, it enters the *renewing* state and begins generating DHCPREQUEST messages as follows:

1. The client transmits a unicast DHCPREQUEST messages to the server that holds the lease.

    If the server is available to receive the message, it responds with either a DHCPACK message, which renews the lease and restarts the lease time clock, or a DHCPNACK message, which terminates the lease and forces the client to begin the address assignment process again from the beginning.

    A DHCPREQUEST to the server that holds the lease is also sent by the client when the client is restarted. If the IP address is available, the lease will be treated like a renewal. If the address is not available, the client receives a DHCPNAK and restarts the lease process.

2. If the server does not respond to the DHCPREQUEST unicast message, the client continues to send them until it reaches the *rebinding time value* or *T2 value,* which defaults to 87.5 percent of the lease period. At this point, the client enters the *rebinding* state and begins transmitting broadcast DHCPREQUEST messages, soliciting an address assignment from any DHCP server on the network.

3. A server can respond with either a DHCPACK or DHCPNACK message.

    If the lease time expires with no response from any DHCP server, the client's IP address is released and all of its TCP/IP communication ceases, except for the transmission of broadcast DHCPDISCOVER messages. The DHCPDISCOVER broadcasts are used to request configuration parameters from a DHCP server.

Manually Releasing, Renewing, and Verifying an IP Address

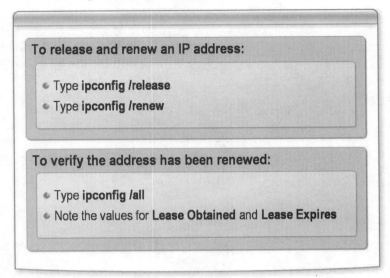

To release and renew an IP address:

- Type **ipconfig /release**
- Type **ipconfig /renew**

To verify the address has been renewed:

- Type **ipconfig /all**
- Note the values for **Lease Obtained** and **Lease Expires**

Introduction

In some instances, you will need to manually release and renew an IP address, and then verify that the address has been renewed. For example, when you need to move a client from one subnet to another and the IP address may not automatically updated.

How to manually release and renew an address

A client can release an IP address at any time by transmitting a DHCPRELEASE message. You can do this manually by using the Ipconfig.exe utility in Windows Server 2003, Windows XP Professional Edition, Windows 2000, and Microsoft Windows NT®.

Note   In Microsoft Windows Me, Microsoft Windows 98, and Microsoft Windows 95, you use the Winipcfg.exe utility.

To manually release and renew an IP address:

1. At the command prompt, type **ipconfig /release** and then press ENTER.

2. Type **ipconfig /renew** and press ENTER again.

How to verify an address

To verify an address has been renewed, either manually or automatically after passing the T1 or T2 time points, and to view the lease expiration date and time, type **ipconfig /all**, press ENTER, and note the values for **Lease Obtained** and **Lease Expires**.

Example of ipconfig/all information

```
Lease Obtained. . . . . . . : Tuesday, May 14, 2003 4:59:26 PM

Lease Expires . . . . . . . : Friday, May 17, 2003 4:59:26 PM
```

Practice: Manually Releasing and Renewing an Address

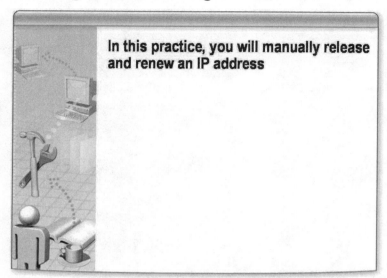

In this practice, you will manually release and renew an IP address

Introduction

In this practice, you will manually release and renew an IP address.

Scenario

A systems engineer has modified DHCP scope settings. A few of the clients have not received the new scope settings. The systems engineer has requested that you release and renew the address leases for those clients.

Practice

► **Release and renew an IP address**

1. Log on as *Computer*User with a password of **P@ssw0rd** (where *Computer* is the name of your computer).

2. Using Run as, open a command prompt as *Computer*\Administrator.

3. At the command prompt, type **ipconfig /all** and press ENTER.

4. Verify that the **DHCP enabled** attribute is **Yes** and that you have an IP address.

5. At the command prompt, type **ipconfig /release** and press ENTER.

   The IP address and subnet mask of your adapter should read **0.0.0.0** You may receive an error message stating the local area connection is unavailable.

6. At the command prompt, type **ipconfig /renew** and press ENTER.

   The IP address and subnet mask of your adapter should be a valid IP address that begins with 192.168.*x*.

7. At the command prompt, type **ipconfig /all** and press ENTER.

8. Note the time of the **Lease Obtained** attribute. What date and time does it show?

   _____

9. Close all windows and log off.

Lesson: Using Alternate Configuration

- How Alternate Configuration Assigns IP Addresses
- How APIPA Assigns IP Addresses

Introduction

Alternate Configuration is a feature of Windows Server 2003 that you can use to streamline multiple-network connectivity. Alternate Configuration is useful when you are using a computer on more than one network and at least one of the networks does not have a DHCP server. Mobile computer users can use Alternate Configuration to automatically assign IP addresses on both office and home networks without having to manually reconfigure TCP/IP settings.

Lesson objectives

After completing this lesson, you will be able to:

- Describe Alternate Configuration.
- Decide which Alternate Configuration method to use.
- Disable Alternate Configuration.

How Alternate Configuration Assigns IP Addresses

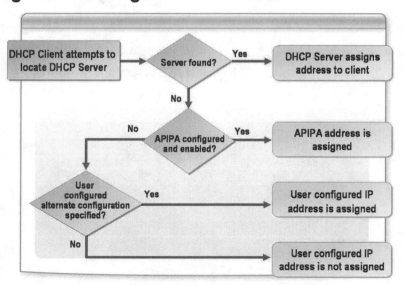

Introduction	Using Alternate Configuration is another way to automatically assign dynamic IP addresses. Understanding how to use Alternate Configuration will help you determine how a client received a particular IP address.

Introduction

Using Alternate Configuration is another way to automatically assign dynamic IP addresses. Understanding how to use Alternate Configuration will help you determine how a client received a particular IP address.

User configured Alternate Configuration

Alternate Configuration provides two methods of automatically assigning an IP address. User configured Alternate Configuration and APIPA.

How to determine which Alternate Configuration method to use

User configured Alternate Configuration provides more detailed parameters than APIPA. In situations where you require a specific IP address and subnet mask for a client, or if you require a default gateway, DNS server, or WINS server, you should use Alternate Configuration. In this case, you must supply the required information for the user configured alternate configuration.

APIPA is most useful in situations where a reserved IP address in the range from 169.254.0.1 through 169.254.255.254 is acceptable, and you do not need access to a default gateway, DNS server, or WINS server.

How Alternate Configuration works

By default, a computer running Windows Server 2003 first tries to contact a DHCP server on the network to dynamically obtain configuration for each installed network connection. When the client contacts the server:

- If a DHCP server is reached and the leased configuration is successful, TCP/IP configuration is completed.

- If a DHCP server is not reached, by default the computer instead uses either APIPA or a user configured alternate configuration to automatically configure TCP/IP.

When specifying a user configured alternate configuration, you may also specify a default gateway, WINS servers, and DNS servers.

The **Alternate Configuration** tab is visible only if **Obtain an IP address automatically** is selected on the **General** tab of the **Internet Protocol (TCP/IP) Properties** dialog box.

How APIPA Assigns IP Addresses

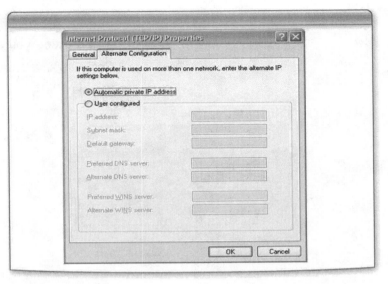

Introduction	APIPA is one of two Alternate Configuration features that you can use to specify an alternate configuration. You only use this method for a network that consists of a single subnet. When you use APIPA, you can create a functioning, single subnet TCP/IP network without having to manually configure the TCP/IP protocol or set up a DHCP server.
What is APIPA?	APIPA is a feature in Windows Server 2003 that automatically configures an IP address. APIPA eliminates errors associated with missing IP addresses that often occur in single-network small office or home office networks that are not connected to the Internet.
How APIPA works	If a DHCP server cannot be reached to assign an IP address automatically and APIPA has been selected as the mode of alternate configuration, Windows Server 2003 selects an address in the reserved IP-addressing class that ranges from 169.254.0.1 through 169.254.255.254 and assigns the subnet mask of 255.255.0.0. This method of obtaining an IP address is termed *Automatic Private IP Addressing*. In this method, DNS, WINS, or a default gateway are not assigned.

Practice: Configuring Alternate Configuration

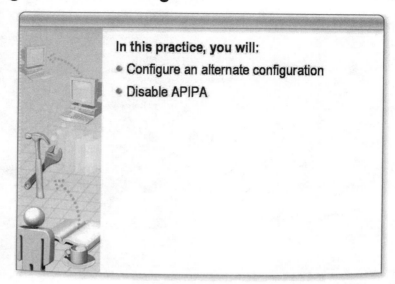

Introduction

In this practice, you will configure a client to use a user-configured Alternate Configuration and disable APIPA.

Scenario

Bob, a laptop user, complains of the difficulty in constantly changing the network configuration when going from work to home and of occasionally receiving an IP address that begins with 169. Bob would like to prevent the 169 address from being assigned to his laptop. While at work, Bob's laptop obtains an IP address using DHCP. At home, Bob's laptop uses a static IP address that Bob must manually configure. You inform Bob that Windows XP has an alternate configuration feature that will allow him to continue network connectivity when going between work and home, without manually reconfiguring the network **Properties** page.

Practice

▶ **Assign a static IP address**

1. Log on as *Computer*\Administrator with a password of **P@ssw0rd** (where *Computer* is the name of your computer).

2. Click **Start**, point to **Control Panel**, point to **Network Connections**, and then click **Local Area Connection**.

   The **Local Area Connection Status** dialog box appears.

3. Click **Properties**.

   The **Local Area Connection Properties** dialog box appears.

4. Click **Internet Protocol (TCP/IP)**, and then click **Properties**.

   The **Internet Protocol (TCP/IP) Properties** dialog box appears.

5. Click the **Alternate Configuration** tab.

6. Click **User Configured**.

7. Use the following tables to complete the Alternate Configuration property page (where *x* is the number of the network).

Computer Name	IP Address
Vancouver	192.168.x.11
Denver	192.168.x.12
Perth	192.168.x.13
Brisbane	192.168.x.14
Lisbon	192.168.x.15
Bonn	192.168.x.16
Lima	192.168.x.17
Santiago	192.168.x.18
Bangalore	192.168.x.19
Singapore	192.168.x.20
Casablanca	192.168.x.21
Tunis	192.168.x.22
Acapulco	192.168.x.23
Miami	192.168.x.24
Auckland	192.168.x.25
Suva	192.168.x.26
Stockholm	192.168.x.27
Moscow	192.168.x.28
Caracas	192.168.x.29
Montevideo	192.168.x.30
Manila	192.168.x.31
Tokyo	192.168.x.32
Khartoum	192.168.x.33
Nairobi	192.168.x.34

Property	Value
IP address	See table above
Subnet mask	255.255.255.0
Default gateway	192.168.x.1
Preferred DNS server	192.168.x.200
Alternate DNS server	192.168.x.201
Preferred WINS server	192.168.x.200
Alternate WINS server	192.168.x.201

8. To close the **Internet Protocol (TCP/IP) Properties** dialog box click **OK**.

9. To close the **Local Area Connection Properties** dialog box, click **Close**.

10. To close the **Local Area Connection Status** dialog box, click **Close**.

▶ **Verify alternate configuration settings**

1. Open a command prompt.

2. Type **ipconfig /all** and press ENTER, locate the **DHCP enabled** attribute. What is its value?

   Yes

3. Locate the **Autoconfiguration Enabled** attribute. What is its value?

   Yes

4. Note the IP address below:

   _192.168.1.50_____

✋ **Wait for your instructor to disable the LONDON network interface.**

5. At the command prompt, type **ipconfig /release** and press ENTER.

6. At the command prompt, type **ipconfig /renew** and press ENTER.

   The following error message is displayed: **An error occurred while renewing interface Local Area Connection: unable to contact your DHCP server. Request has timed out.**

7. At the command prompt, type **ipconfig /all** and press ENTER.

8. Locate the **IP address** attribute.

   How does the attribute read?

9. Locate the **DHCP enabled** attribute.

   What is its value?

10. Locate the **Autoconfiguration enabled** attribute.

    What is its value?

✋ **Wait for your instructor to enable the LONDON network interface.**

▶ **Disable APIPA on the entire computer**

1. Click **Start**, click **Run**, type **regedit** and then click **OK**.

2. Use Registry Editor to navigate to the following registry key:

   ```
   HKEY_LOCAL_MACHINE\SYSTEM\CurrentControlSet\Services\Tcpip\
   Parameters
   ```

3. On the **File** menu, click **Export**.

4. In the **File name** box, type **c:\tcpip_parameters** and click **Save**.

   A copy of the registry key is exported. Use this to restore the key if necessary.

5. On the **Edit** menu, point to **New,** and then click **DWORD Value**.

6. Type **IPAutoconfigurationEnabled** and press ENTER.

Note   Registry keys are often case-sensitive. Be sure to type the key exactly as shown.

---

7. Verify that **0x00000000 (0)** appears in the data column.

8. Close Registry Editor.

Note   If the IPAutoconfigurationEnabled entry is not present, a default value of 1 is assumed, which indicates that APIPA is enabled.

---

9. Restart the computer using the information in the following table.

Parameter	Value
Option	Operating System: Reconfiguration (Planned)
Comment	Disabled APIPA

▶ **Verify Alternate Configuration is disabled**

1. Log on as *Computer*\Administrator with a password of **P@ssw0rd** (where *Computer* is the name of your computer).

2. Open a command prompt, type **ipconfig/all** and press ENTER.

3. Locate the **Autoconfiguration enabled** attribute.

   What is its value?

   No

Wait for your instructor to disable the LONDON network interface.

4. At the command prompt, type **ipconfig /release** and press ENTER.

5. At the command prompt, type **ipconfig /renew** and press ENTER.

   The following error message is displayed: An error occurred while renewing interface local Area Connection: unable to contact your DHCP server. Request has timed out.

6. At the command prompt, type **ipconfig /all** and press ENTER.

7. Locate the **IP address** attribute.

   How does the attribute read? *10.2.146.N.12*

▶ **Renew the client's IP address**

Wait for your instructor to enable the London network interface.

1. At the command prompt, type **ipconfig /renew** and press ENTER.

2. Verify that you have received an IP address.

   192.168.1...

Course Evaluation

Your evaluation of this course will help Microsoft understand the quality of your learning experience.

At a convenient time before the end of the course, please complete a course evaluation, which is available at http://www.CourseSurvey.com.

Microsoft®
Training &
Certification

Module 4: Configuring a Client for Name Resolution

Contents

Overview

- **Resolving Client Names**
- **Managing the ARP Cache**
- **Overview of NetBIOS**
- **Using Static Name Resolution**
- **Using Dynamic Name Resolution**
- **Summarizing the Name Resolution Process**

Introduction

As part of the Microsoft® Windows® Server 2003 installation process, you specify a name by which the computer is known to the network. The Windows Setup program refers to this as a computer name, and it is used to generate other names such as a Network Basic Input/Output System (NetBIOS) name and Domain Name System (DNS) host name. To use NetBIOS names on a Transmission Control Protocol/Internet Protocol (TCP/IP) network, there must be mechanisms that resolve the names into Internet Protocol (IP) addresses and then to media access control (MAC) addresses needed for TCP/IP communication. This module describes the various types of name resolution mechanisms provided by the Windows operating systems and how to use them for clients on your network.

Note In this module, the term *client* refers to a computer running a Windows operating system on a network running TCP/IP. The term *host* includes clients and refers to any device on the network that has an IP address.

Objectives

After completing this module, you will be able to:

- Describe how client names are resolved.
- Describe how Address Resolution Protocol (ARP) resolves client MAC addresses.
- Describe the function of NetBIOS.
- Configure a client to use a static IP address.
- Configure a client to use a dynamic IP address.
- Configure a client to use name resolution servers.

Lesson: Resolving Client Names

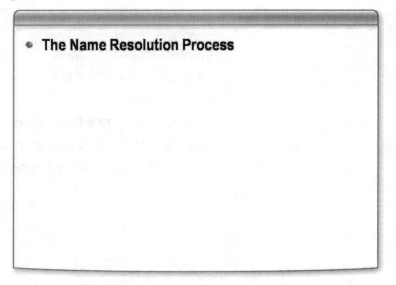

- **The Name Resolution Process**

Introduction

You must configure the client computers on your network so that their computer names can be resolved into IP addresses. When you configure clients for name resolution, you are ensuring that they can communicate with other computers using computer names. For two hosts to communicate on a network, the MAC address of each host must be identified. An IP address is associated with a MAC address, and a computer name is associated with an IP address. Name resolution is the process of obtaining the IP address associated with the computer name. Knowing the various methods for resolving computer names assists you in performing these administrative tasks successfully.

Lesson objective

After completing this lesson, you will be able to describe how client names are resolved to IP addresses.

Multimedia: The Name Resolution Process

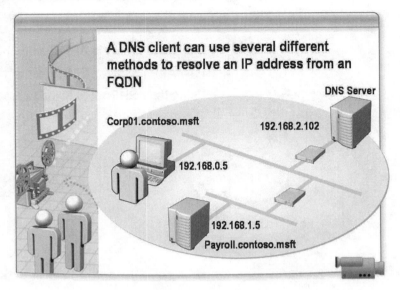

File location

To view the multimedia presentation, *The Name Resolution Process*, open the Web page on the Student Materials compact disc, click **Multimedia**, and then click the title of the presentation.

Objective

Upon completion of this presentation, you will be able to describe the methods a DNS client can use to resolve an IP address from a fully qualified domain name (FQDN).

Lesson: Managing the ARP Cache

- Static and Dynamic ARP Cache Entries
- How ARP Resolves IP Addresses to MAC Addresses
- Using the ARP Tool to Manage the ARP Cache

Introduction

Each network adapter has a unique and permanent MAC address, also known as a physical address, which corresponds to one or more IP addresses associated with the adapter. The MAC address is used as a final destination address, and it must be resolved from the IP address so that the computer can receive data. You use ARP, which is a TCP/IP protocol, to resolve MAC addresses. To ensure that ARP is functioning correctly, you must know how ARP works and how to manage ARP entries.

Lesson objectives

After completing this lesson, you will be able to:

- Recognize static and dynamic ARP cache entries.
- Describe how ARP resolves IP addresses to MAC addresses.
- Use the ARP tool to manage the ARP cache.
- Modify the ARP cache.

Static and Dynamic ARP Cache Entries

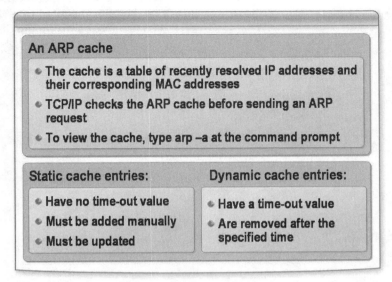

An ARP cache
- The cache is a table of recently resolved IP addresses and their corresponding MAC addresses
- TCP/IP checks the ARP cache before sending an ARP request
- To view the cache, type arp –a at the command prompt

Static cache entries:
- Have no time-out value
- Must be added manually
- Must be updated

Dynamic cache entries:
- Have a time-out value
- Are removed after the specified time

Introduction

ARP performs IP address-to-MAC address resolution for outgoing packets of data. The packet includes the source and destination IP address. Each outgoing packet is encapsulated in a frame, at which time source and destination MAC addresses must be added. ARP determines the destination MAC address for each frame.

The ARP cache

To minimize the amount of broadcast network traffic that ARP generates, the computer stores recently resolved IP addresses and their corresponding MAC addresses in a cache. The information remains in the cache for a short period of time, usually between 2 and 10 minutes, in case the computer has additional packets to send to the same address. TCP/IP checks the cache before sending out a broadcast request to obtain a MAC address.

Static cache entries

Windows Server 2003 includes a command-line utility called Arp.exe that you can use to view and manipulate the contents of the ARP cache. For example, you can use Arp.exe to add the MAC addresses of computers you contact frequently to the cache, thus saving time and network traffic during the connection process. Addresses that you add manually are static, meaning that they are not deleted after the usual expiration period. The cache is stored in memory, however, so it is erased when you restart the computer. It is rarely necessary to add static routes to the ARP cache. However, you might temporarily add a route to troubleshoot a network connectivity issue.

Adding routes incorrectly is likely to disrupt network communication to the host identified in the entry.

Note If you want to preload the cache when you start your system, you can create a batch file containing Arp,exe commands and execute it from the Windows Startup group. However, you must update these cache entries when computers are added to, or removed from, your network.

Dynamic cache entries   Dynamic entries are added to the cache during the ARP resolution process. Dynamic entries have a time-out value associated with them to remove them from the cache after a specific amount of time. Dynamic ARP cache entries for Windows Server 2003 are given a maximum time-out value of ten minutes.

How to view the ARP cache   To view the ARP cache on a Windows Server 2003–based computer, type **arp -a** at the command prompt.

How ARP Resolves IP Addresses to MAC Addresses

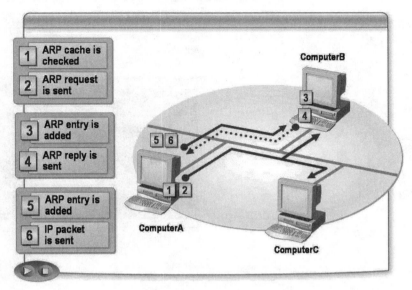

Introduction

Before transmitting an IP packet, TCP/IP clients must resolve the forwarding or next-hop IP address to its corresponding MAC address. If the MAC address for the next-hop is not in the ARP cache, the client will broadcast an ARP request frame to obtain the MAC address. The computer using that IP address responds with an ARP reply message containing its MAC address. With the information in the reply message, the computer can encapsulate the IP packet in the appropriate frame and transmit it to the next-hop.

The ARP process

In the proceeding illustration, ComputerA is broadcasting an ARP request to ComputerB and ComputerC. The following steps describe the process:

1. On ComputerA, ARP consults its own ARP cache for an entry for the destination IP address. If an entry is found, ARP proceeds to step 6.

2. If an entry is not found, ARP on ComputerA builds an ARP Request frame containing its own MAC address and IP address and the destination IP address. ARP then broadcasts the ARP Request.

3. ComputerB and ComputerC receive the broadcasted frame and the ARP Request is processed. If the receiving computer's IP address matches the requested IP address (the destination IP address), its ARP cache is updated with the address of the sender of the ARP Request, ComputerA.

    If the receiving host's IP address does not match the requested IP address, as in the case of ComputerC, the ARP Request is discarded.

4. ComputerB formulates an ARP Reply containing its own MAC address and sends it directly to ComputerA.

5. When ComputerA receives the ARP Reply from ComputerB it updates its ARP cache with the IP address and MAC address.

    ComputerA and ComputerB now have each other's IP to MAC address mappings in their ARP caches.

6. ComputerA sends the IP packet to ComputerB.

Using the ARP Tool to Manage the ARP Cache

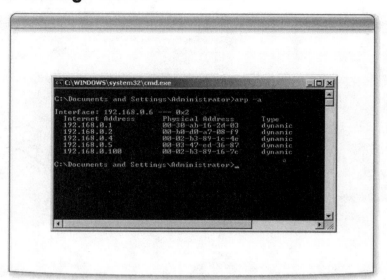

Introduction

You can use the ARP tool to view and modify entries in the local ARP cache. The ARP cache, which is a memory-resident list, contains one or more tables that store IP addresses and the corresponding MAC addresses that have been resolved from other computers on the same subnet. A separate table exists for each network adapter installed on the computer.

How to use ARP to isolate connection issues

You can use the ARP tool to isolate connections issues. For example, if two computers on the same subnet cannot communicate with each other, you can use ARP to determine if the correct MAC addresses are listed. To verify the MAC addresses are correctly listed in the ARP cache, you run the **arp -a** command on each computer. This displays the IP and MAC addresses listed in the ARP cache for each computer. You verify the MAC address listed in the ARP cache is the same as the actual MAC address for the destination computer by using Ipconfig.exe.

Example of output from the arp –a command

The following example shows the output for the **arp -a** command, which displays the ARP cache tables for all network interfaces.

```
C:\>arp -a
Interface: 172.16.0.142 on Interface 0x2
Internet address      Physical address      Type

172.16.0.1            00-e0-34-c0-a1-40      dynamic
172.16.1.231          00-00-f8-03-6d-65      Dynamic
172.16.3.34           08-00-09-dc-82-4a      Dynamic
172.16.4.53           00-c0-4f-79-49-2b      Dynamic
172.16.5.102          00-00-f8-03-6c-30      Dynamic
```

How to use the arp –a command

To display the ARP cache table specifically for the interface that is assigned the IP address 172.16.1.231, type **arp -a -N 172.16.1.231**

The **arp -a** command is also useful for determining whether the IP protocol is properly associated, or bound, to the network adapter. If it is not, the command shows an empty ARP cache. To determine bindings for the network adapter you are currently using, use the **ipconfig /all** command.

ARP syntax and parameters

ARP uses the following syntax:

arp [**-a** [*InetAddr*] [**-N** *IfaceAddr*]] [**-g** [*InetAddr*] [**-N** *IfaceAddr*]] [**-d** *InetAddr* [*IfaceAddr*]] [**-s** *InetAddr EtherAddr* [*IfaceAddr*]]

The following table describes the function of the ARP parameters.

Parameter	Function
-a	Displays current ARP cache entries for all interfaces. To display the ARP cache entry for a specific IP address, type **arp -a** *InetAddr*, where *InetAddr* is an IP address.
-N	Lists ARP entries for the interface specified by -N *IfaceAddr*, where *IfaceAddr* is the IP address assigned to the interface. The -N parameter is case sensitive.
-g	Displays the current ARP entries for all interfaces if no *InetAddr* is specified. To display the ARP cache entry to a specific IP address, type **arp -g** *InetAddr*.
-d	Removes an entry specified by its IP address (*InetAddr*) from the ARP cache. To remove an entry for a specific interface, type **arp -d** *IfaceAddr*, where *IfaceAddr* is the IP address assigned to that interface. To delete all entries, use the asterisk (*) wildcard in place of *InetAddr*.
-s	Adds a static entry to the ARP cache that resolves the specified IP address (*InetAddr*) to the MAC address (*EtherAddr*). To add a static ARP cache entry to the table for a specific interface, type **arp -s** *IfaceAddr*, where *IfaceAddr* is the IP address assigned to that interface.
/?	Displays ARP parameters.

Practice: Identifying a MAC Address

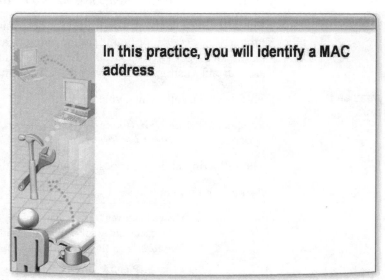

In this practice, you will identify a MAC address

Introduction

In this practice, you will identify the MAC address of your computer and the MAC address of the instructor computer.

Scenario

You are isolating connectivity issues and want to determine the MAC addresses of two computers.

Practice

▶ **Identify the MAC address of the local computer**

1. Log on to your computer with your *Computer*User account (where *Computer* is the name of your computer), and with a password of **P@ssw0rd**

2. Open a command prompt, type **ipconfig /all** and press ENTER.

3. Locate the Physical Address attribute.

   The physical address value is your MAC address.

▶ **Identify the MAC address of a remote computer on your network**

1. At the command prompt type **ping 192.168.*x*.200** where *x* is the network number for the classroom, and press ENTER.

2. After receiving a successful reply, type **arp –a** and press ENTER.

3. Locate the physical address for 192.168.*x*.200. This is the MAC address for 192.168.*x*.200.

4. Close the command prompt.

Practice: Viewing and Modifying the ARP Cache

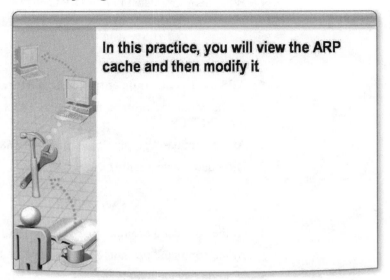

In this practice, you will view the ARP cache and then modify it

Introduction

In this practice, you will clear the ARP cache, use the Ping utility (Ping) on a client computer, and add an invalid ARP cache entry to determine the impact of an incorrect MAC address.

Scenario

You use Ping to test, or *ping* a remote computer and do not receive a reply. You decide to determine whether the ARP cache has the correct MAC address associated with the router's IP address. You determine that the MAC address for the router is incorrect and decide to add a static ARP cache entry.

Practice

▶ **Clear the ARP cache and add a dynamic entry**

1. Using Run as, open a command prompt as *Computer*\Administrator (where *Computer* is the name of your computer), type **arp –d *** and press ENTER.

   The specified entry was not found reply will be displayed if the ARP cache is already cleared.

2. To view the contents of the ARP cache, type **arp –a** and press ENTER.

3. What items are listed?

   nothing

4. Type **ping 192.168.x.200** and press ENTER.

5. Did you receive a reply?

   yes

6. Type **arp –a** and press ENTER.

7. What items are listed in the ARP cache?

admin

▶ **Add an invalid static entry to the ARP cache and then remove it**

1. At the command prompt, type **arp –s 192.168.x.200 11-11-11-11-11-11** and press ENTER.

2. At the command prompt, type **ping 192.168.x.200** and press ENTER.

3. Did you receive a reply?

No timeout

4. At the command prompt, type **arp –d *** and press ENTER.

5. At the command prompt, type **ping 192.168.x.200** and press ENTER.

6. Did you receive a reply?

Yes

7. At the command prompt, type **arp –a** and press ENTER.

8. Is there an entry for 192.168.x.200?

Yes

Lesson: Overview of NetBIOS

- The Types of Names Computers Use
- What Is NetBIOS?
- What Is a NetBIOS Name?
- What Is NetBT?
- Types of NetBT Nodes
- What Is Nbtstat?

Introduction

NetBIOS acts to connect applications together in the session and transport layers of TCP/IP, providing messaging and resource allocation. NetBIOS establishes logical names on the network, establishes sessions between two logical names on the network, and supports reliable data transfer between computer that have established a session. Understanding how NetBIOS functions in a network will assist you in understanding network communications.

Lesson objectives

After completing this lesson, you will be able to:

- Describe the types of names computers use.
- Describe the function of NetBIOS.
- Determine the NetBT node type.
- Use Nbtstat.

The Types of Names Computers Use

Name	Description
NetBIOS Names	• 16-byte address • Can represent a single computer or group of computers • 15 characters used for the name • 16th character is used by the services that a computer offers to the network
Host Names	• Assigned to a computer's IP address • 255 characters in length • Can contain alphabetic and numeric characters, hyphens, and periods. • Can take various forms • Alias • Domain name

Introduction

TCP/IP identifies source and destination computers by their IP addresses. However, computer users are much better at remembering and using names than numbers, so common, or user-friendly names are assigned to the computers IP address. These names are either NetBIOS names or host names.

Note Microsoft Windows 2000 and Windows Server 2003 do not require NetBIOS names; however, previous versions of Windows require NetBIOS to support networking capabilities.

NetBIOS name

A NetBIOS name is a 16-character name that is used to identify a NetBIOS resource on the network. A NetBIOS name can represent a single computer or a group of computers The first 15 characters may be used for the name. The final character is used to identify the resource or service that is being referred to on the computer.

An example of a NetBIOS resource is the File and Printer Sharing for Microsoft Networks component on a computer running Windows Server 2003. When your computer starts, this component registers a unique NetBIOS name, based on the name of your computer and character identifier that represents the component.

Host name

A host name is a user-friendly name that is assigned to a computer's IP address to identify it as a TCP/IP host. The host name can be up to 255 characters in length and can contain alphabetic and numeric characters, hyphens, and periods. Host names can take various forms. The two most common forms are alias and domain name. An alias is a single name associated with an IP address, such as *payroll*. A domain name is structured for use on the Internet and includes periods as separators. An example of a domain name is *payroll.contoso.com*.

What Is NetBIOS?

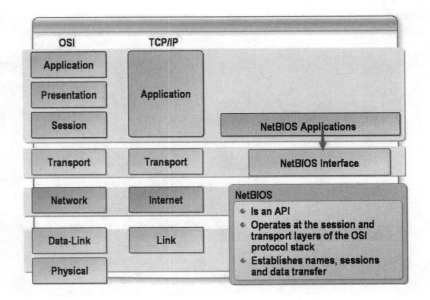

Introduction

NetBIOS is a specification created by IBM and Microsoft that allows distributed applications to access each other's network services independent of the transport protocol being used. It integrates with TCP/IP, running at the session and transport levels.

NetBIOS establishes names on the network, establishes sessions between two named services on the network, and supports reliable data transfer between computers that have established a session.

Definition of NetBIOS

NetBIOS provides network input/output services to support client/server applications on a network. From an architectural viewpoint, the NetBIOS specification defines:

- An interprocess communication (IPC) mechanism and application programming interface (API) that allows applications that are NetBIOS-enabled to communicate remotely over a network and request services from lower levels of the TCP/IP protocol stack. This is the primary and original definition of NetBIOS.

- A protocol operating at the session and transport layers of the Open Systems Interconnection (OSI) reference model that enables functions such as session establishment and termination as well as name registration, name renewal, and name resolution.

Note For more information about the TCP/IP and OSI models, see Module 1, "Reviewing the Suite of TCP/IP Protocols," in Course 2276A, *Implementing a Microsoft Windows Server 2003 Network Infrastructure: Network Hosts*.

What Is a NetBIOS Name?

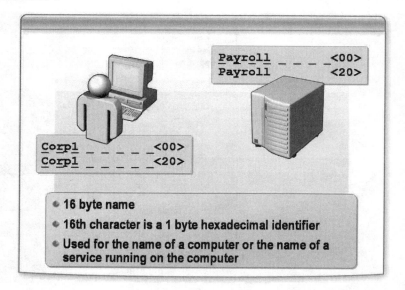

Introduction

Each service that is NetBIOS-enabled requires a NetBIOS name to identify it on the network. This NetBIOS name consists of a name assigned to the computer during installation that can be up to fifteen characters, along with a sixteenth character that identifies the type of service or function that is being referred to on the computer.

NetBIOS names are registered dynamically when computers and services start and when users log on. The NetBIOS name space is flat, meaning that names can be used only once within a network

How NetBIOS names are constructed

The fifteen-character name can include the computer name, the domain name, or the name of the user who is logged on. You must add spaces if needed to total fifteen characters. The sixteenth character is a 1-byte hexadecimal identifier.

For example, the sixteenth character identifying the Windows Server 2003 Messenger service has the 1-byte hexadecimal identifier 03h. On a computer running Windows Server 2003 named SERVER12   (Note the extra spaces make the name fifteen characters long), the Messenger service would be uniquely identified on the network with the NetBIOS name SERVER12   [03h]. NetBIOS names are also distinguished by whether they are:

■ A unique name, which applies to a single IP address.

■ A group name, which applies to multiple IP addresses.

■ A multihomed name, which apples to a group of IP addresses assigned to a single host.

Common Suffixes for NetBIOS Names

The following table shows some of the more common suffixes that constitute the hidden sixteenth character of a NetBIOS name and the networking service with which they are associated.

Suffix (Hex)	First 15 Characters	Networking Service
00	Computer name	Workstation service
00	Domain name	Domain name
03	Computer name	Messenger service
03	User name	Messenger service
20	Computer name	File Server service
1B	Domain name	Domain master browser
1C	Domain name	Domain controllers
1D	Domain name	Master browser
1E	Domain name	Browser service election

Tip   To view the NetBIOS names registered for your computer, use the **nbtstat –n** command.

What Is NetBT?

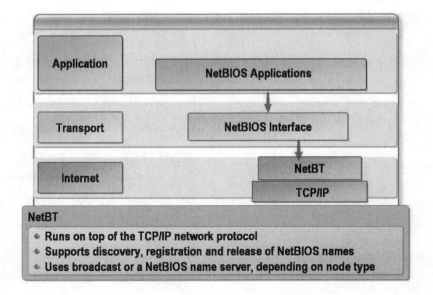

Introduction

By default, NetBIOS names do not function over a TCP/IP network. Windows Server 2003 enables NetBIOS clients to communicate over TCP/IP by providing the NetBIOS over TCP/IP (NetBT) protocol. By using this protocol, you are ensuring that NetBIOS-based applications can use TCP/IP to provide NetBIOS network services to NetBIOS applications. To effectively provide network communication between NetBIOS applications and hosts, you must understand NetBIOS naming functions.

What NetBT does

NetBT is the NetBIOS session-layer protocol and APIs running on top of TCP/IP. NetBT supports NetBIOS sessions, NetBIOS datagrams and naming functions such as the discovery, resolution, and release of NetBIOS names on a TCP/IP network.

How NetBIOS determines the method for naming functions

There are several ways that NetBT can perform naming functions. For example, NetBT can use a broadcast, or use a NetBIOS Name Server (NBNS) such as a Microsoft Windows Internet Name Service (WINS) server, or use both. The node type of the network device determines how NetBIOS naming functions are performed. Node refers to any uniquely addressable device on a network. The node type also determines the order in which the functions are performed.

The following list describes the NetBIOS naming functions:

- NetBIOS name resolution:

  NetBT hosts that want to communicate with similar hosts must issue a NetBIOS name query request to resolve the NetBIOS name to its IP address.

- NetBIOS name registration:

  NetBT hosts must register their unique NetBIOS names when they are initialized on a network to ensure that there are no duplicate names on the network. NetBIOS name registration can be done either by broadcasts or by unicast messages sent to a WINS server. Either or both methods can be used, and in either order, depending on the NetBT node type of the host.

- NetBIOS name release:

  NetBT hosts must release their NetBIOS names when they are shut down or when a particular NetBIOS-enabled service is stopped on the server. This enables the released name to be used by another host. NetBIOS name release can be done by broadcasts or by unicast messages sent to a WINS server. Either or both methods can be used in either order, depending on the NetBT node type of the host.

Types of NetBT Nodes

NetBt Node Types	
B-node (broadcast)	Uses NetBIOS broadcast name queries
P-node (peer-to-peer)	Uses NBNS
M-node (mixed)	A combination of B-node and P-node. Uses broadcast by default
H-node (hybrid)	A combination of B-node and P-node. Uses NBNS by default
Microsoft enhanced B-node	Uses the Lmhosts file

Introduction

The method that NetBT applies to perform naming functions depends on the node type of the client.

NetBT Node Types

The NetBT node types are listed in the following table.

Node Type	Method (in the Order Applied)	Comments
B-node (broadcast)	Broadcast only	Uses broadcast NetBIOS name queries for name registration and name resolution. Typically not forwarded by routers, so limited to local subnet. Can create excessive broadcast traffic for large subnets.
P-node (peer-to-peer)	NBNS only	Uses NBNS
M-node (mixed)	Broadcast, NBNS	A combination of B-node and P-node. Uses broadcast by default. If unable to resolve, uses NBNS.
H-node (hybrid)	NBNS, Broadcast	A combination of P-node and B-node. Uses NBNS by default. Default node type for Microsoft clients if an NBNS is configured on the network.
Microsoft enhanced B-node	NetBIOS name cache, Broadcast, Lmhosts file	An enhanced broadcast that utilizes the Lmhosts file. Default node type for Microsoft clients if no NBNS is configured on the network.

Tip   You can configure the NetBIOS node type on a client running Microsoft Windows Server 2003 by using the registry, but the preferred way is to configure Dynamic Host Configuration Protocol (DHCP) to specify the node type to the client.

Practice: Determining and Setting the NetBT Node Type of a Client

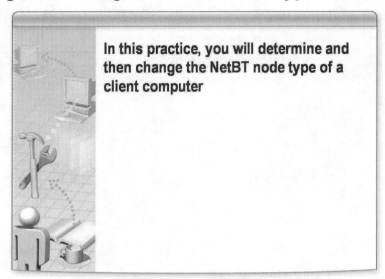

In this practice, you will determine and then change the NetBT node type of a client computer

Introduction

In this practice, you will determine and set the NetBT node type of the client.

Scenario

You are isolating NetBIOS name resolution issues. You have been asked to change the node type to b-node for a computer on a network segment that is unable to reach a name server.

Practice

▶ **Determine the NetBT node type of your computer**

1. At the command prompt, type **ipconfig /all** and press ENTER.

2. Locate the Node Type label. What is the NetBT node type?

hybrid

▶ **Set the node type using a batch file**

1. At the command prompt, type **cd c:\moc\2276\labfiles** and press ENTER.

2. Type **node p** and press ENTER.

3. Type **ipconfig /release** and press ENTER.

4. Type **ipconfig /renew** and press ENTER.

5. Type **ipconfig /all** and press ENTER.

6. Locate the Node Type label. What is the NetBT node type?

peer to peer

7. To return the node type to Hybrid, type **node h** and press ENTER.

8. Type **ipconfig /release** and press ENTER.

9. Type **ipconfig /renew** and press ENTER.

10. Type **ipconfig /all** and press ENTER.

11. Verify that Node Type is Hybrid.

What Is Nbtstat?

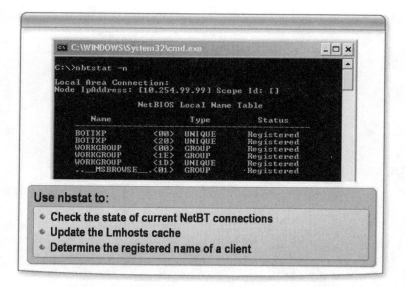

Use nbstat to:

• Check the state of current NetBT connections
• Update the Lmhosts cache
• Determine the registered name of a client

Introduction

Nbtstat is a TCP/IP utility that displays information about the NetBT connections that Windows uses when communicating with other Windows computers on the TCP/IP network. Nbtstat is installed on a computer running Microsoft Windows Server 2003 by default.

What nbtstat displays

Nbtstat displays NetBT protocol statistics, NetBIOS name tables for both the local computer and remote computers, and the NetBIOS name cache. The NetBIOS name table is the list of NetBIOS names that corresponds to NetBIOS applications running on that computer. You can use Nbtstat to refresh the NetBIOS name cache and the names registered with WINS.

How to use nbtstat

You can use nbtstat to:

- View NetBT statistics on the computer.

- Determine the status of the computer's current network connections.

- Preload entries in an Lmhosts file into the NetBIOS name cache.

- View the NetBIOS name of a computer.

- Isolate NetBIOS name resolution issues.

To use nbtstat, run **nbtstat** from the command prompt.

Examples of nbtstat displays

nbtstat -n displays the NetBIOS names of the host that have been registered on the system;

nbtstat -c displays the current contents of the NetBIOS name cache, which contains NetBIOS name to IP address mappings for other hosts on the network.

Tip   You can run nbtstat -a < ComputerName > to obtain the local NetBIOS name table on <ComputerName> and its MAC address.

Lesson: Using Static Name Resolution

- Using an Lmhosts File
- Guidelines for Configuring a Client to Use Lmhosts
- Using a Hosts File

Introduction

When users on your network specify a user-friendly name to communicate with a destination computer, TCP/IP requires an IP address for transmission to occur, so the computer name is resolved, or mapped to an IP address. This mapping is then stored in either a static or dynamic table, or in both tables. In a static table, mappings for NetBIOS names are stored in the Lmhosts file, and mappings for host names are stored in the Hosts file, or in both files.

The advantage of using a static table is that, because it is a text file located on each computer, it is easy for you to customize. You can create any number of required entries, including easy-to-remember aliases or nicknames for frequently accessed resources. However, it is difficult to maintain and update static tables if the tables contain a large number of IP address mappings, or if the IP addresses change often.

Lesson objectives

After completing this lesson, you will be able to:

- Add an entry to an Lmhosts file.
- Add an entry to a Host file.

Using an Lmhosts File

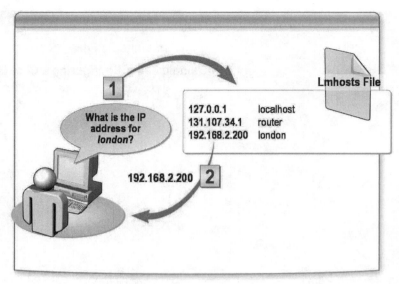

Introduction

Windows Server 2003 enables you to map NetBIOS names manually to IP addresses by using the Lmhosts file. By using the Lmhosts file, you can reduce the number of IP broadcasts. Selected mappings from the Lmhosts file are maintained in a limited cache of mappings. This memory cache is local to the client computer and is initialized when the computer is started.

How the Lmhosts file resolves names

The name resolution process is as follows:

1. When the computer needs to resolve a name, the cache is examined first.

2. If there is no match in the cache, Windows Server 2003 uses broadcast NetBIOS Name Query request messages to try to find the NetBIOS computer.

3. If the IP broadcast name queries fail, the computer parses the complete Lmhosts file in addition to the cache to find the NetBIOS name and the corresponding IP address. In this way, the Lmhosts file can contain many mappings without requiring a large amount of static memory to maintain an infrequently used cache.

4. If the computer cannot resolve the name by using the Lmhosts file, the computer uses DNS for name resolution.

How to use the Lmhosts file

You can use the Lmhosts file to map computer names and IP addresses for computers outside of the local subnet; for example, you can use the Lmhosts file to find remote computers for network file, print, and remote procedure services. You can also use the Lmhosts file to locate domain controllers performing domain services such as logging on, browsing, and replication.

Before configuring a computer to use the Lmhosts file, you must create the primary Lmhosts file local to each computer, name the file Lmhosts, and save the file in the *systemroot*\System32\Drivers\Etc folder.

Because the Lmhosts file is a simple text file, you can create and change the Lmhosts file by using a text editor, such as Microsoft Notepad.

Caution   An example Lmhosts file named Lmhosts.sam is provided in the Windows Server 2003 *systemroot*\System32\Drivers\Etc folder. This is only an example file. Do not use this file as the primary Lmhosts file.

Guidelines for Configuring a Client to Use Lmhosts

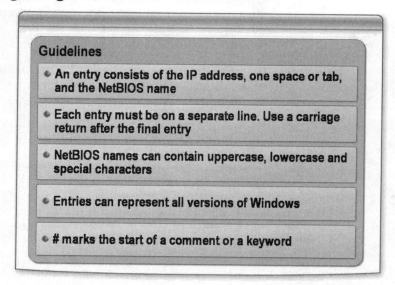

Guidelines

- An entry consists of the IP address, one space or tab, and the NetBIOS name

- Each entry must be on a separate line. Use a carriage return after the final entry

- NetBIOS names can contain uppercase, lowercase and special characters

- Entries can represent all versions of Windows

- # marks the start of a comment or a keyword

Introduction

There are no exact rules for configuring a client to use Lmhosts, however, there are guidelines you should follow to make sure that you configure the client correctly.

Guidelines for configuring a client to use Lmhosts

Use the following guidelines to create and edit entries in the Lmhosts file:

- To create an entry, use the IP address of the computer, followed by at least one space or tab and the NetBIOS name of the computer.

  > **Caution** You should not add an Lmhosts entry for a computer that is a DHCP client because the IP addresses of DHCP clients change dynamically. To avoid problems, make sure that the computers for which names are entered in the Lmhosts files are configured with static IP addresses.

- You must place each entry on a separate line. Add a carriage return after the final entry in the file.

- You can use uppercase and lowercase characters and special characters in NetBIOS names. If a name is placed between double quotation marks, it is used exactly as entered. For example, *AccountingPDC* is a mixed-case name, and *HumanRscSr   \0x03* specifies a name with a special character.

- Entries in the Lmhosts file can represent computers that are running Windows Server 2003 and earlier, as well as Microsoft LAN Manager and Microsoft Windows for Workgroups version 3.11 with Microsoft TCP/IP. There is no need to distinguish between different platforms in the Lmhosts file.

- Use the pound sign (#) to mark the start of a comment. You can also use # to designate special keywords. For example, #PRE which will cause the entry to be preloaded into the NetBIOS name cache.

Note For information about the keywords that you can use in the Lmhosts file, see "Creating Entries in the LMHOSTS File" in Appendix H of the *Microsoft Windows Server 2003 Resource Kit*.

Practice: Adding an Entry to the Lmhosts File

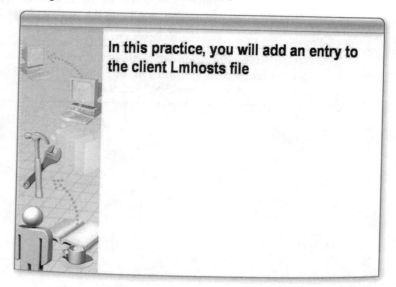

In this practice, you will add an entry to the client Lmhosts file

Introduction

In this practice, you will add an entry to an Lmhosts file, purge and reload the NBT Remote cache table, and verify that your entry has been loaded.

Scenario

You are isolating connectivity issues on a client computer and want to force NetBIOS name resolution using an Lmhosts file to preload a name into the NetBIOS name cache.

Practice

▶ **Purge and view the contents of the NBT Remote cache**

1. At the command prompt, type **nbtstat –R** and press ENTER.

    A message is displayed stating the purge and preload of the NBT Remote Cache Name Table was successful.

2. Type **nbtstat –c** and press ENTER.

3. Record the entries, if any, below:

    _____

▶ **Create review the sample Lmhosts file and add an entry to it**

1. Click **Start**, point to **All Programs**, point to **Accessories**, right-click **Notepad** and then click **Run as**.

2. Click **Run as** and then click **The following user**.

3. In the **User name** box, verify that *Computer*\Administrator appears.

4. In the **Password** box, type **P@ssw0rd** and click **OK**.

5. On the **File** menu, click **Open**.

6. In the **Files of type** box, select **All Files**.

7. In the **File name** box, type **%windir%\system32\drivers\etc** and press ENTER.

8. Right-click **lmhosts.sam** and click **Rename**.

9. Delete ".sam" from the end of the file name, press ENTER, and then press F5.

10. Click **lmhosts** and then click **Open**.

11. Review the contents of the file.

    The Lmhosts sample file contains information about how to create an lmhosts file.

12. On the **Edit** menu, click **Select all** and press the DELETE key.

13. At the first line of the file, type **192.168.x.200 MyLondon #PRE**

14. Save and close the Lmhosts file.

▶ **Purge and re-load the Lmhosts file into the NBT Remote cache**

1. At the command prompt, type **nbtstat –R** and press ENTER.

2. Type **nbtstat –c**, press ENTER, and then record the entries below:

   London nwtrader <b37   uniqe   IP   465

Using a Hosts File

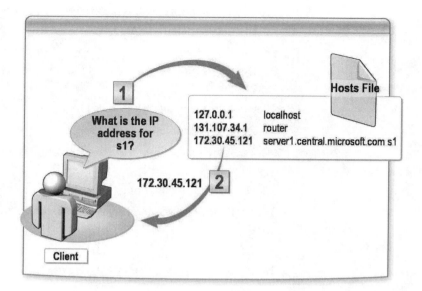

Introduction

A Hosts file is a text file that provides a local method for resolution of host names into their respective IP addresses on a TCP/IP network. You can use Hosts files as an alternative to DNS servers, or together with DNS servers to resolve names on your TCP/IP network. You use a Hosts file on a small network or when it is not practical to maintain a DNS server.

Example of a table in the Hosts file

The following is a table of IP addresses and host names.

```
127.0.0.1          localhost
131.107.34.1       router
172.30.45.121      server1.central.microsoft.com s1
```

Note that the server at the IP address 172.30.45.121 can be referred to by either its FQDN, *server1.central.microsoft.com*, or the nickname, *s1*. Using a nickname allows a user to refer to the server without typing the entire FQDN.

Guidelines for using the Hosts file

Use the following guidelines to create and edit entries in the Hosts file:

- You can assign multiple host names to the same IP address.

- Entries in the Hosts file for Windows Server 2003 and Windows 2000 are not case sensitive.

- To create an entry, use the IP address of the computer followed by the FQDN. You can complete the entry with a comment. You use the pound sign (#) as a prefix for this optional comment.

- To locate the Hosts file, use the appropriate path as follows:

  - Microsoft Windows NT®, Windows 2000, and Windows XP:

    %SystemRoot%\system32\ drivers\etc\Hosts

  - Microsoft Windows 95 or Windows 98:

    \%WinDir%\Hosts

Common causes of Hosts file issues

Connectivity issues associated with Hosts file are commonly caused by one or more of the following:

- The Hosts file does not contain the particular host name.
- The host name in the Hosts file or in the command is misspelled.
- The IP address for the host name in the Hosts file is invalid or incorrect.
- The Hosts file contains multiple entries for the same host on separate lines. Because the Hosts file is parsed from the top, the first entry found is used.

Tip   Place the host names that need to be most frequently resolved near the top of the Hosts file, as the file is parsed linearly from the beginning.

Practice: Adding an Entry to the Hosts File

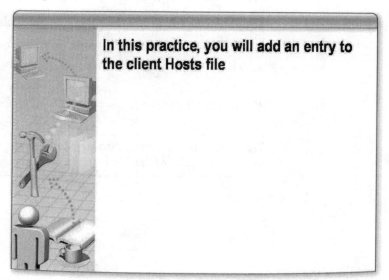

In this practice, you will add an entry to the client Hosts file

Introduction

In this practice, you will add an entry to a Hosts file.

Scenario

A client is unable to connect to a remote computer by its host name. The client is using a Hosts file for name resolution, and you have been asked to verify it and update it if necessary.

Practice

▶ **Simulate the connectivity problem**

1. At the command prompt, type **ping mocinstructor** and press ENTER.

2. Did you receive a reply?

▶ **Add an entry to a Hosts file**

1. Using Run as open Notepad.exe as *Computer*\Administrator.

2. On the **File** menu, click **Open**.

3. In the **File name** box, type **c:\windows\system32\drivers\etc\hosts** and then click **Open**.

4. Add a new line at the end of the file, type **192.168.*x*.200 mocinstructor** and then press ENTER.

5. Save and close the Hosts file.

6. At the command prompt, type **ping mocinstructor** and then press ENTER.

7. Did you receive a reply?

Lesson: Using Dynamic Name Resolution

- **What Is WINS?**
- **What Is DNS?**
- **The DNS Suffix**

Introduction

The advantage of using dynamic tables to store IP mappings is that the tables are updated automatically. To accomplish this, you use two Windows Server 2003 services: WINS and DNS. These services perform the same functions as the Lmhosts and Hosts files, but relieve you of the need to configure the files manually.

Lesson objectives

After completing this lesson, you will be able to:

- Describe WINS.
- Describe DNS.
- Use Ipconfig to manage the DNS client resolver cache.
- Configure a client to use a name server.

What Is WINS?

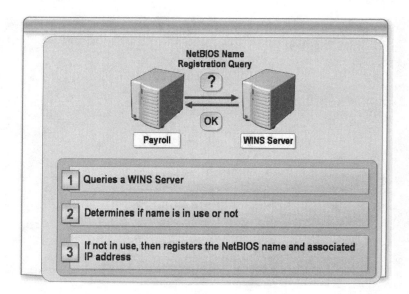

Introduction

WINS is a NBNS that you can use to resolve NetBIOS names to IP addresses when computers on your network are running Microsoft Windows Server 2003, Windows 2000, Windows NT 4.0, Windows 98, or Windows 95.

Benefits of using WINS

WINS provides a centralized database for registering dynamic mappings of NetBIOS names used on a network. WINS is built on a protocol that registers, resolves, and releases NetBIOS names by using unicast transmissions, rather than repeated transmissions of broadcast messages. This protocol allows the system to work across routers and eliminates the need for an Lmhosts file, restoring the dynamic nature of NetBIOS name resolution and allowing the system to work seamlessly with DHCP. For example, when dynamic addressing through DHCP creates new IP addresses for computers that move between subnets, the WINS database tracks the changes automatically.

Note   WINS supports the NetBT mode of operation defined in Request for Comments (RFC) numbers 1001 and 1002 as p-node.

The WINS name resolution process

WINS is the Microsoft implementation of a NetBIOS name server. For WINS to function properly on a network, each client must:

- Register its NetBIOS name in the WINS database. When a client starts up, it will register its name with its configured WINS server.

- Renew its name registration at intervals. Client registrations are temporary, and from time to time a WINS client must renew its name or its lease will expire.

- Release names from the database when shutting down. When a WINS client no longer requires a name, for example when it is shut down, the client sends a message instructing the WINS server to release its name.

After it is configured with WINS as a name resolution method, the client will also use WINS to perform NetBIOS name queries. It does the following:

1. If the client cannot resolve the name from its cache, it sends a name query to its primary WINS server. If the primary WINS server does not respond, the client sends the request two more times.

2. If the client does not receive a response from its primary WINS server, the client resends the request to any additional WINS servers configured at the client. If a WINS server resolves the name, it responds to the client with the IP address of the requested NetBIOS name.

3. If no response is received, or if a Name not found message is received from the WINS server, the client then moves on to its next configured name resolution method.

What Is DNS?

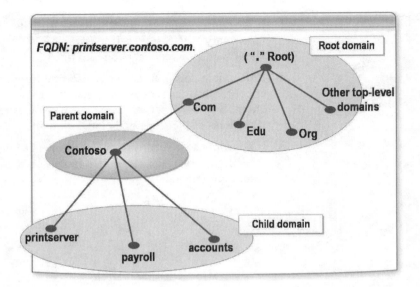

Introduction	DNS provides a distributed database that is used to resolve FQDNs and other host names to IP addresses. All server versions of Windows 2003 include a DNS Server service. When you use DNS, you are enabling users on your network to apply user-friendly names, instead of IP addresses, to network resources.
How DNS resolves names to IP addresses	DNS uses a database of names and IP addresses to provide this service. DNS client software performs queries and updates to the DNS database. A user trying to locate a print server can use the DNS name *printserver.contoso.com*, for example, and have that name resolved to an IP address such as 172.16.23.55.
The DNS resolver cache	When DNS receives a positive response to a query, it adds that response to its client resolver cache. DNS always checks the cache before querying any other DNS servers. If a name is in the cache, DNS uses the name rather than querying other servers. This expedites queries and decreases network traffic for DNS queries.

Note For more information about DNS, see RFCs 1034 and 1035 under **Additional Reading** on the Student Materials compact disc.

The DNS namespace	The schema of the DNS database groups information about network resources into a hierarchical structure of alphanumeric *domains*. The hierarchical structure of domains is an inverted tree structure beginning with a *root domain* at its apex and descending into separate branches with common levels of *parent domains* and downward further into singular *child domains*. The representation of the entire hierarchical domain structure is known as a DNS *namespace*.

A DNS namespace may be created in any TCP/IP network by hosting the DNS root domain on a DNS server, but each DNS namespace must be separate from all other DNS namespaces as they are separate hierarchies. The DNS namespace on the Internet is the most common DNS namespace, but you may create a separate DNS namespace within your network with its own root domain that is entirely unrelated to the Internet DNS namespace. As may be expected, configuring hosts in separate DNS namespaces so that they can locate each other is complicated and requires separate devices such as proxy servers.

DNS nodes

Each name in the DNS namespace is typically called a node. A DNS node, such as *ftp.contoso.com*, could represent a DNS domain, a host name, or a network service.

How DNS differs from WINS

DNS database records are replicated among DNS servers. The extensible nature and consequent size of the DNS database, along with the need to support frequent updates from multiple sources, requires that the DNS database be maintained in a distributed manner among DNS servers. In contrast, a WINS server is a flat database. Because WINS is a flat database it cannot be distributed and therefore does not have the scalability of a DNS database. Each DNS server hosts a portion of the DNS database and responds to queries for names in that portion with authoritative answers and then stores its answers in a cache. This local caching of query resolution information is used to improve performance.

Note For more information about DNS and the domain namespace, see Module 5, "Configuring DNS for Host Name Resolution," in Course 2277A, *Implementing, Managing, and Maintaining a Microsoft Windows Server 2003 Network: Network Services*.

The DNS Suffix

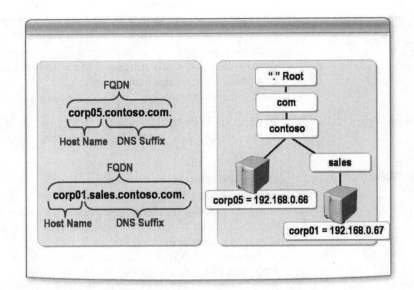

Introduction	In Windows Server 2003, you can enable users to locate and access a computer as identified by its FQDN using DNS.
The FQDN	The FQDN is a DNS name that uniquely identifies the computer on the network. By default, it is a concatenation of the host name, the primary DNS suffix, and a period. For example, an FQDN might be *corp01.sales.contoso.com*.
Primary DNS suffix	The primary DNS suffix name is the same as the domain name specified during installation of Windows Server 2003 and listed in **System Properties**. You can view the primary DNS suffix for your computer from the **Computer Name** tab of **System Properties**.

The primary DNS suffix is also known as the primary domain name. For example, the FQDN corp05.contoso.com. has the primary DNS suffix contoso.com. |
| **Connection-specific DNS suffix** | You can apply connection-specific DNS suffixes to the separate network adapter connections used by a *multihomed* computer to identify the host when it is connected to separate networks using different domain names. A multihomed computer is a computer with two or more network interfaces, such as network interface adapters. When using a connection-specific DNS suffix, a full computer name is also a concatenation of the host name and a connection-specific DNS suffix. For example, a connection-specific DNS suffix might be *sales.contoso.com*.

The connection-specific DNS suffix is also known as an adapter-specific DNS suffix. |
| **Full computer name** | The full computer name is a concatenation of the single-label host name, such as *corp01*, and a multi-label primary DNS suffix name, such as *sales.contoso.com*. Using the host and primary DNS suffix examples, the full computer name is *corp01.sales.contoso.com*. The host name is the same as the Computer Name specified during the installation of Windows Server 2003. |

Practice: Using Ipconfig to Manage the DNS Client Resolver Cache

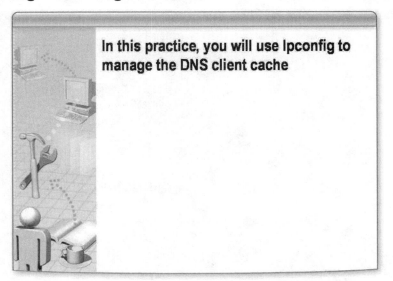

In this practice, you will use Ipconfig to manage the DNS client cache

Introduction

In this practice, you will use Ipconfig to display and clear the DNS client resolver cache.

Scenario

You are isolating client connectivity issues that seem to involve incorrect DNS name resolution. You suspect that an expired entry is present in the client resolver cache and decide to clear it.

Practice

▶ **View the DNS client resolver cache**

1. At the command prompt, type **ipconfig /displaydns** and press ENTER.

2. Observe the DNS entries displayed. You may need to scroll up in the command window.

3. Type **ipconfig /flushdns** and press ENTER.

4. A message appears stating the cache was successfully flushed.

5. Type **ipconfig /displaydns** and press ENTER.

6. What entries are displayed?

   mocinstrvt local first

7. Close all windows and log off.

Practice: Configuring a Client to Use a Name Server

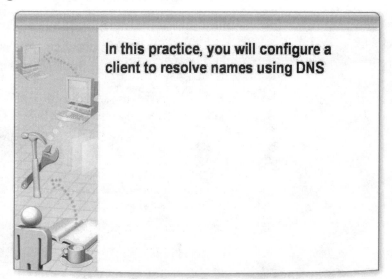

In this practice, you will configure a
client to resolve names using DNS

Introduction

In this practice, you will configure the DNS client to use static DNS and WINS server addresses by using the Local Area Connections property sheet. This configuration would need to be performed on all computers that require Internet or intranet access where DHCP is not used.

Scenario

Your organization is opening a new satellite office that will have only 15 workstations and a router to connect to the Internet. This router will also be used to connect to the corporate network, but will continue using the same DNS server configuration. Because there will be no DHCP services in use by this office, you must configure static IP addresses and static DNS server addresses.

Practice

▶ **Document your current Internet Protocol TCP/IP settings**

1. Log on as administrator with a password of **P@ssw0rd**.

2. Open a command prompt, type **ipconfig /all** and then press ENTER.

3. Document your current TCP/IP settings:

   a. IP address   192.168.1.50

   b. Subnet mask   255.255.255.0

   c. Default gateway   192.168.1.200

   d. DNS servers   192.168.1.200

   e. Primary WINS server   192.168.1.200

▶ **Configure the local area connection to use a static TCP/IP address**

1. Click **Start**, point to **Control Panel**, point to **Network Connections**, and then click **Local Area Connection**.

2. Click **Properties**.

3. Click **Internet Protocol (TCP/IP)**, and then click **Properties**.

4. Click **Use the following IP address**, and then use the settings that you documented in the previous procedure.

5. In the **Use the following DNS server addresses** section, enter the DNS server addresses that you documented in the previous procedure.

6. Click **OK** to accept the new settings, click **Close** to close the **Local Area Connection Properties** dialog box, and then click **Close** to close the **Local Area Connection Status** dialog box.

7. At the command prompt, type **ipconfig /all** and then press ENTER.

8. Verify that settings match those recorded in the previous procedure.

▶ **Configure the local area connection to use a WINS server**

1. At the command prompt, locate the Primary WINS Server attribute. Is it displayed?

   yes

2. Click **Start**, point to **Control Panel**, point to **Network Connections**, and then click **Local Area Connection**.

3. Click **Properties**.

4. Click **Internet Protocol (TCP/IP)**, and then click **Properties**.

5. On the **General** tab, click **Advanced**.

6. Click **WINS**, and then click **Add**.

7. In the **TCP/IP WINS Server** dialog box, type **192.168.x.200** and then click **Add**.

8. To close the **Advanced TCP/IP Settings** dialog box, click **OK**.

9. To close the **Internet Protocol (TCP/IP) Properties** dialog box, click **OK**.

10. To close the **Local Area Connection Properties** dialog box, click **Close**.

11. To close the **Local Area Connection Status** dialog box, click **Close**.

12. At the command prompt, type **ipconfig /all** and press ENTER.

13. Does the Primary WINS Server attribute appear?

    yes

14. Close all windows and log off.

Lesson: Summarizing the Name Resolution Process

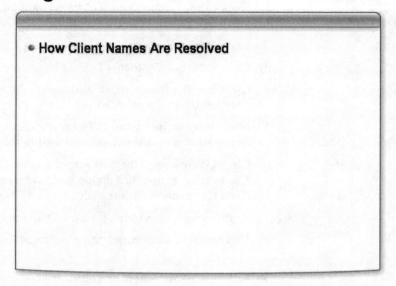

- How Client Names Are Resolved

Introduction   TCP/IP identifies source and destination computers by their IP addresses. Name resolution methods attempt to determine the IP address associated with a name.

Objective   After completing this lesson, you will be able to describe the process of resolving client names to IP addresses.

How Client Names Are Resolved

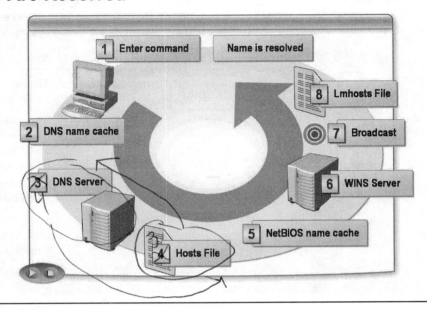

Introduction	For hosts on your network to communicate with each other, their user-friendly names must be resolved to IP addresses.
What is name resolution?	Name resolution is the process by which the user-friendly name of a computer is resolved to its IP address on a TCP/IP network. Name resolution enables hosts to communicate with each other by using TCP/IP. After a host's name has been resolved to its IP address, ARP can then be used to resolve the next hop IP address into its corresponding MAC address. After the MAC address of the next hop address is known, frames may be placed on the network.
Name resolution in Windows	For clients running Windows Server 2003, Windows 2000, and Windows XP, you primarily use DNS to resolve names. Clients running previous versions of Windows primarily use NetBIOS names for network communication. As a result, these clients require a method of resolving NetBIOS names to IP addresses.
How it works	When you go to the command prompt of a machine running Microsoft Windows and type a Net Use command to map a drive to a network shared folder, you can type the NetBIOS name of the target host in the command. For example, *net use x: \\servername\sharename.* For this command to be fulfilled, the NetBIOS name of the remote host must first be resolved into its IP address so that it can be contacted on the network. This process is called NetBIOS name resolution.

You can use a number of different methods to perform NetBIOS name resolution. By default, a Windows Server 2003–based computer that is not configured as a WINS client or WINS server uses broadcast mode for name resolution.

Each method is successively tried until the name is resolved into its IP address or name resolution fails. Some methods will not be available—for example, when there is no NBNS or DNS server on the network.

Example of NetBIOS name resolution

The following table shows the order in which methods of name resolution are attempted when the NetBT node type of the client is H-node, **Enable Lmhosts Lookup** is checked on the **WINS** tab of **Advanced TCP/IP Properties** and **Enable DNS** registry setting is set to 1, as described in the following table.

Method in the order applied	Comments
1. Check local NetBIOS name cache	The cache contains recently resolved NetBIOS names.
2. Contact NBNS	This method works only if NBNS is configured. WINS is usually the NBNS on a Microsoft network. The requestor tries three times to contact the name server, and then tries three times to contact a secondary WINS server if there is one.
3. Perform local broadcast	The requestor broadcasts a NetBIOS name query request packet. The requestor tries three times before giving an error.
4. Check local Lmhosts file	The requestor checks if an Lmhosts file exists.
5. Check DNS client cache	The requestor checks its DNS client cache for the name.
6. Check local hosts file	On Windows Server 2003, the requestor checks the Hosts file if **Enable DNS For Windows Resolution** is selected on the **WINS Address** tab of the TCP/IP property sheet. This option is not available for Windows 2000.
7. Contact DNS server (if all methods fail, an error message states that the computer could not be found on the network)	The requestor contacts the DNS server if **Enable DNS For Windows Resolution** is selected on the **WINS Address** tab of the TCP/IP property sheet and the **DNS** tab has a DNS server specified on it. The requestor also tries 5, 10, 20, and 40 seconds later.

Note   The name resolution process stops when the first IP address is found for the name.

Microsoft®
Training &
Certification

Module 5:
Isolating Common
Connectivity Issues

Contents

Overview

- ● Determining the Causes of Connectivity Issues
- ● Network Utilities That You Can Use to Isolate Connectivity Issues

Introduction

The information in this module introduces you to a process for isolating common connectivity issues, and also describes how you can use network utilities and tools as part of this process. To maintain network connectivity, you must be able to isolate issues that interrupt it. When you isolate connectivity issues, you are assisting systems engineers in resolving these issues as rapidly as possible.

Objectives

After completing this module, you will be able to:

- ■ Employ a method to systematically resolve connectivity issues.
- ■ Use utilities and a job aid to isolate common connectivity issues.

Lesson: Determining the Causes of Connectivity Issues

- What Are the Common Connectivity Issues?
- Before You Begin Isolating the Issue
- Isolating the Issue
- Resolving the Issue
- After the Issue Is Resolved

Introduction

One of the key elements in isolating a network problem is using a consistent, effective strategy for determining the cause. Many of the trouble calls that you receive will be due to user errors that can be resolved through a little training for the user. When you are faced with a more complex complaint, however, you should follow a set procedure for isolating and resolving the issue.

Lesson objectives

After completing this lesson, you will be able to:

- Describe the common connectivity issues.
- Make time-saving preparations before starting to isolate a problem.
- Follow the issue isolation procedure to the source of a problem.
- Make a plan for implementing a solution.
- Hold a post-resolution meeting and document the actions that led to the solution.

What Are the Common Connectivity Issues?

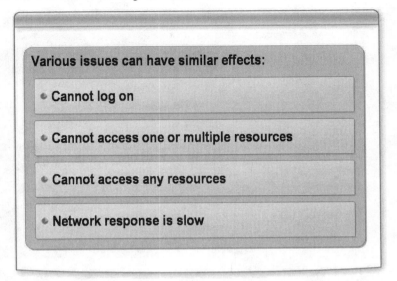

Various issues can have similar effects:

- Cannot log on
- Cannot access one or multiple resources
- Cannot access any resources
- Network response is slow

Introduction

As a systems administrator, you will not be able to personally resolve every issue that occurs on your network. However, you should be able to isolate the source of an issue, and to determine whether it is one that you can fix or something that you need to escalate to an expert.

Common issues

Most issues will be presented to you by users who find that they are unable to perform a specific action at their computers—either something that they were able to do previously or something that they think they should be able to do presently.

There are only a few basic types of complaints:

- User cannot log on.
- User cannot access either one resource or multiple resources.
- User cannot access *any* resources.
- Network response is slow.

A single basic problem may have a wide variety of causes. For example, a user who cannot log on may simply be entering the wrong password; or all the domain controllers may be offline; or the cause could lie in any of a large number of locations in between. Isolating the problem may be a long and complex process—or it may only take a minute—depending on the cause. The challenge for you is to isolate the single cause from the many possibilities.

Before You Begin Isolating the Issue

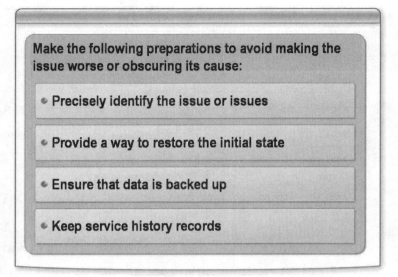

Make the following preparations to avoid making the issue worse or obscuring its cause:

- Precisely identify the issue or issues
- Provide a way to restore the initial state
- Ensure that data is backed up
- Keep service history records

Introduction

If you think that an issue will require a large effort to resolve, you can save yourself time by making preparations that will help you to both proceed as efficiently as possible and avoid making the problem worse.

Precisely identify the issue or issues

It can be difficult to determine the exact nature of an issue from the description given by a user. That is why the first action of the isolation is to obtain accurate information about what has occurred.

To help identify the issue or issues, ask the following questions:

- What exactly were you doing when the problem occurred?
- Was the computer operating normally just before the problem occurred?
- Has the problem occurred before?
- Have you had any other problems?
- Has any hardware or software been installed, removed, or reconfigured recently?
- Did you or anyone else make any changes while trying to resolve the problem?

Provide a way to restore the initial state

Before changing the configuration of a computer or other device, note its original settings. This can include:

- Noting the client's network configuration, which includes the Internet Protocol (IP) address, the default gateway's IP address, and the subnet mask.
- Noting what services are set to automatic, but are not running.
- Reviewing the event log for errors that are already occurring before you change the configuration.
- Using the Ping utility to determine the level of connectivity to the gateway and remote computers before you start.

If disabling a feature or changing a setting does not produce the results that you want, use your notes to restore the feature or setting before trying another solution. Not restoring settings can cause new problems and can also make it difficult to determine which of your actions caused a particular effect.

Ensure that data is backed up

Backups are important for computers of all sizes, from clients to high-availability servers. If you suspect that your efforts to isolate a problem might worsen the situation, or that the situation presents any risk to important data, then perform a backup before you make any changes. This enables you to restore the system if you lose data, cause Stop errors, or create startup problems.

Your backup should include the following items:

- The user's personal folder that is located in the Documents and Settings folder. This includes the My Documents folder and folders that contain personalization information such as the user's Favorites list and Desktop settings.

- The system state, which includes the registry and other vital system files.

Note   A quick way to back up important client data is by using the Backup or Restore Wizard that is included with Microsoft® Windows® XP. To start the wizard, in **Performance and Maintenance**, in Control Panel, click **Back up your data**.

After you make the backup, consider performing the following steps to check that the data is written correctly to the backup media:

- Use the verification option provided by your backup software.

- Restore a few files from the backup media.

Keep service history records

To detect trends and patterns in your network's performance, you should record each service action that is performed. If you have a small network, you could simply keep the records in a notebook but larger networks require a more versatile solution.

A useful way to store large numbers of records is to use a database management system to create a service history database with a record for each device on your network. Using a database enables you to search across all your records for similar types of problems or occurrences during a specific time period.

Regardless of the medium on which it is stored, each record should start with baseline performance information gathered when the host was added to the network. Update the baseline information after installing new hardware or software so you can compare past and current behavior and performance levels.

Your service history records should include the:

- Baseline performance data.
- Dates and times of problems and resolutions.
- Changes that you made.
- Reasons for the changes.
- Name of the person who made the changes.
- Positive and negative affects the changes had on the stability and performance of the client and network.
- Information provided by technical support.

Note For more information about creating a configuration management database, see the Information Technology Infrastructure Library (ITIL) and Microsoft Operations Framework (MOF) Web links provided on the Student Materials compact disc.

Isolating the Issue

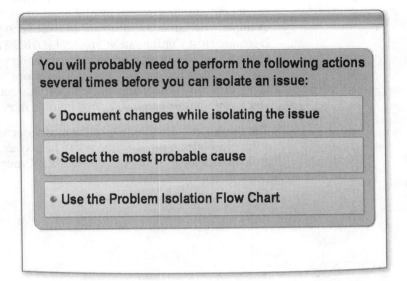

You will probably need to perform the following actions several times before you can isolate an issue:

• Document changes while isolating the issue

• Select the most probable cause

• Use the Problem Isolation Flow Chart

Introduction	Locating the source of a problem may be a long and an arduous process, or it may take only a few minutes. In either case, the Problem Isolation Flow Chart can help you to identify the shortest path to a solution.
Document changes while isolating the issue	Documenting the steps you take while troubleshooting will help you review your actions after you resolve the problem. This is useful for very complex problems that require lengthy procedures to resolve. Documenting your steps:

- Helps you to verify that you are neither duplicating nor skipping steps.

- Allows others to assist you with the problem.

- Enables you to evaluate the effectiveness of your efforts.

- Makes it possible for you to identify the exact steps to take, if the problem should ever recur.

Begin documenting your actions at the start of issue isolation, rather than waiting until after you have finished and then attempting to remember all the steps that you took.

Select the most probable cause	When you look for the causes of a problem, begin with the most obvious possibilities. For example, if a client is unable to communicate with a file server, do not begin by checking the routers between the two systems. Check the simple things on the client first—such as whether the network cable is connected to the computer.

Use the Problem Isolation Flow Chart

The Problem Isolation Flow Chart is located in Appendix C. It begins with simple logon problems and progresses in complexity through problems with client configuration, names resolution, routers, firewalls, and other servers. For example, you can use it to isolate an issue such as a single client not obtaining a Dynamic Host Configuration Protocol (DHCP) address. Following the decision tree, you avoid spending time troubleshooting specific applications or devices such as routers and bridges that apply to more than one computer. Since you know this issue is only applicable to a single computer, the flowchart directs you away from isolation tasks that involve more than one computer.

The flowchart helps you to take the most effective steps in the most logical order to isolate an issue. Using it will help you to determine whether the problem is a local issue that you can fix by yourself, or a broader problem that you will need to escalate.

Resolving the Issue

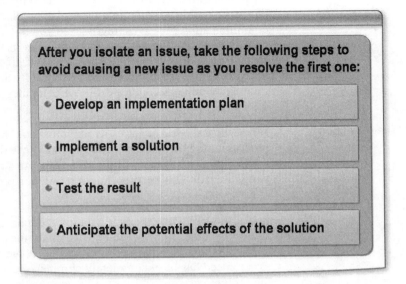

| Introduction | After you have isolated the source of an issue, you must decide how to resolve it. You can probably fix a simple problem on a client immediately. A larger issue, such as a problem that involves multiple servers that serve hundreds of clients, could require help and cooperation from several groups in your organization. |

Introduction

After you have isolated the source of an issue, you must decide how to resolve it. You can probably fix a simple problem on a client immediately. A larger issue, such as a problem that involves multiple servers that serve hundreds of clients, could require help and cooperation from several groups in your organization.

Develop an implementation plan

After you identify the problem and find a solution that has been tested on one or more computers, you might need an implementation plan if the solution will be deployed across your organization, possibly involving hundreds or thousands of computers. Coordinate your plan with managers and staff members in the affected areas to verify that the schedule does not conflict with important activities.

Your plan can include:

■ Estimates of the time and resources that will be needed.

■ Provisions for troubleshooting during off-peak work hours.

■ A schedule to divide the work into stages over the necessary period.

■ Substitute hardware, if the failing equipment performs a vival role, to be used until the equipment can be fixed.

As the number of users grows; the potential loss of productivity due to disruption increases. Your plan must account for dependencies, allow for last-minute changes, and include contingency plans for unforeseen circumstances.

Implement a solution

After you have isolated the problem to a particular piece of equipment, you can try to determine whether it is being caused by hardware or software. If it is a hardware problem, you might try replacing the unit that is at fault. For example: communication problems might force you to try replacing network cables until you find one that is faulty. If the problem is in a server, you might need to replace components (such as hard drives) until you find the failing piece. If you determine that the problem is caused by software, you can try storing data or running an application on a different computer, or try reinstalling the software on the client that has the problem.

Test the resolution

When the issue has been resolved, you should return to the beginning of the process and repeat the task that originally revealed the problem. If the problem no longer occurs, test all of the other functions that are related to the changes that you made, this ensures that in fixing one problem you did not create a new one.

It is at this point that the time you spent documenting the isolation process shows its value. You should repeat exactly the procedures that you used to duplicate the problem, to ensure that the problem the user originally experienced has been completely eliminated and not just temporarily masked. If the problem was intermittent to begin with, it may take some time to ascertain whether your solution has been effective. You might need to check with the user several times to make sure that the problem is not reoccurring.

Anticipate the potential effects of the solution

It is important, throughout the troubleshooting process, to keep an eye on the big network picture, and not to let yourself become too involved in the problems experienced by only one user. It is sometimes possible, while implementing a solution to one problem, to create another problem that is more severe or that affects more users.

For example, if users on one subnet are experiencing high traffic levels that reduce their client performance, you might be able to remedy the problem by connecting some of their computers to a different subnet. However, although this solution might help the users with the original problem, you might overload another subnet in the process, causing a new problem that is more severe than the first one. You could consider a more far-reaching solution instead, such as creating a new subnet and then moving some of the affected users to that new subnet.

After the Issue Is Resolved

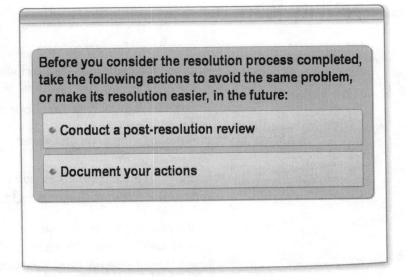

Before you consider the resolution process completed, take the following actions to avoid the same problem, or make its resolution easier, in the future:

- Conduct a post-resolution review

- Document your actions

Introduction

When the network is functioning normally again, it is a good investment of time to review and document just what has happened, in order to avoid (or at least to minimize the impact of) similar problems in the future.

Conduct a post-resolution review

Starting with your compiled documentation, conduct a post-troubleshooting review with the concerned parties, during which they can help you to pinpoint troubleshooting areas that need improvement. Some questions that you might ask during this self-evaluation period include:

- What changes resulted in improvements?
- What changes made the problem worse?
- Was system performance restored to expected levels?
- What work was redundant or unnecessary?
- How effectively were technical support resources used?
- What utility or information was not used that might have helped?
- What unresolved issues require further root-cause analysis?

When it is practical, you should also explain to the user both *what* happened, and *why* it happened. The most important aspect of this conversation is letting the user know whether their actions caused the problem, exacerbated it, or made it more difficult to resolve. Such conversations can make the resolution of future issues significantly easier.

Compile your notes

The final phase of resolving the issue is to condense your notes and documentation into a concise description of both the problem and its resolution for inclusion in your service history database.

Lesson: Network Utilities That You Can Use to Isolate Connectivity Issues

- Address Resolution Utilities Included with TCP/IP
- Other Utilities Included with TCP/IP
- Using the Ping Utility to Test Connectivity to a Remote Host
- Interpreting Ping Error Messages
- Variations on Ping
- Features of the Network Connections Repair Option
- How to Use Network Diagnostics to Gather System Information
- Features of the Netsh Command
- How to Access Netsh Contexts
- How to Use the Netsh Command to Configure a Network Interface Adapter

Introduction

Windows Server 2003 automatically installs most of the utilities that you need for isolating network problems when you install the operating system. There are several additional utilities that you can install from the Windows Server 2003 compact disc (CD) when you need them.

Lesson objectives

After completing this lesson, you will be able to:

- Use the network utilities that you need for isolating connectivity issues.
- Analyze the output from the utilities to help you isolate connectivity issues.

Address Resolution Utilities Included with TCP/IP

The following address resolution command-line utilities are included with TCP/IP:

- Use ARP to check IP to MAC address conversion
- Use Nbtstat to check NetBIOS name to IP address resolution
- Use Nslookup to check DNS name to IP address resolution

Introduction

You can use three of the utilities included with the Transmission Control Protocol / Internet Protocol (TCP/IP) to test whether IP addresses are being converted to MAC addresses, Network Basic Input/Output System (NetBIOS) names are being converted to IP addresses, and Domain name System (DNS) names are being converted to IP addresses.

Use Arp to check IP to MAC address conversion

The Address Resolution Protocol (ARP) converts IP addresses to the MAC addresses that data-link layer protocols require in order to transmit frames. To minimize the amount of network traffic ARP generates, the client stores the resolved hardware addresses in a cache in system memory. The information remains in the cache for a short period of time (usually between 2 and 10 minutes), in case the computer has additional packets to send to the same address.

The Arp utility is used to manipulate the contents of the ARP cache. For example, you can use Arp.exe to add to the cache the hardware addresses of hosts that you contact frequently, thus saving both time and network traffic during the connection process. Addresses that you add to the cache manually are static, meaning that they are not deleted after the usual expiration period. The cache is stored in memory only, however, so it is erased each time that you restart your client.

If you want to preload the cache whenever you start your client, you can create a batch file containing Arp.exe commands, and execute the batch file from the Windows Startup group.

Net stat

Arp.exe uses the following syntax:

```
ARP [-a {ipaddress}] [-n ipaddress] [-s ipaddress hwaddress
{interface}] [-d ipaddress {interface}]
```

- **-a** *{ipaddress}* This parameter displays the contents of the ARP cache. The optional *ipaddress* variable specifies the address of a particular cache entry to be displayed.

- **-n** *ipaddress* This parameter displays the contents of the ARP cache, where *ipaddress* identifies the network interface for which you want to display the cache.

- **-s** *ipaddress hwaddress {interface}* This parameter adds a new entry to the ARP cache, where the *ipaddress* variable contains the IP address of the client, the *hwaddress* variable contains the hardware address of the same client, and the *interface* variable contains the IP address of the network interface in the local system for which you want to modify the cache.

- **-d** *ipaddress {interface}* This parameter deletes the entry in the ARP cache that is associated with the host represented by the *ipaddress* variable. The optional *interface* variable specifies the cache from which the entry should be deleted.

An ARP table as displayed by Arp.exe, appears as follows:

```
Interface: 192.168.2.6 on Interface 0x1000003
  Internet Address    Physical Address      Type
  192.168.2.10        00-50-8b-e8-39-7a     dynamic
  192.168.2.99        08-00-4e-a5-70-0f     dynamic
```

Use Nbtstat to check NetBIOS to IP address resolution

You can use the Nbtstat command-line utility to isolate NetBIOS name resolution problems. For example, use **nbtstat –n** to determine whether a specific NetBIOS name is registered.

When a network is functioning correctly, NetBIOS over TCP/IP (NetBT) resolves NetBIOS names to IP addresses. NetBT uses several options for NetBIOS name resolution, including local cache lookup, Windows Internet Naming Service (WINS) server query, broadcast, LMHOSTS lookup, HOSTS lookup, and DNS server query.

You can use Nbtstat to display a variety of information, including:

- NetBT protocol statistics.

- NetBIOS name tables both for the local client and for remote hosts. The NetBIOS name table is the list of NetBIOS names that corresponds to NetBIOS applications running on the client.

- The contents of the NetBIOS name cache. The NetBIOS name cache is the table that contains NetBIOS name–to–IP address mappings.

You can also use Nbtstat to refresh both the NetBIOS name cache and the names registered with WINS. The following output is an example of output created by using Nbtstat:

```
C:\Documents and Settings\Administrator>nbtstat -c

Local Area Connection:
Node IpAddress: [192.168.0.5] Scope Id: []

                    NetBIOS Remote Cache Name Table

    Name                Type        Host Address      Life [sec]
    -----------------------------------------------------------------
    MYLONDON      <03>  UNIQUE      192.168.0.200       -1
    MYLONDON      <00>  UNIQUE      192.168.0.200       -1
    MYLONDON      <20>  UNIQUE      192.168.0.200       -1
```

Use Nslookup to check DNS name to IP address resolution

Nslookup enables you to generate DNS request messages and also to transmit them to specific DNS servers on the network. Use Nslookup to determine what IP address a particular DNS server has associated with a host name. The basic syntax of nslookup is as follows:

NSLOOKUP *DNSname DNSserver*

- *DNSname* Specifies the DNS name that you want to resolve.

- *DNSserver* Specifies the DNS name or IP address of the DNS server that you want to query for the name specified in the *DNSname* variable.

The output generated by the utility looks like the following sample.

```
C:\>nslookup microsoft.com
Server:  dns1.rcsntx.sbcglobal
Address:  151.164.1.8

Non-authoritative answer:
Name:    microsoft.com
Address:  207.46.249.222
```

The output sample shows that when queried, the dns1.rcsntx.sbcglobal.net DNS server returns 207.46.249.222 as the IP address associated with microsoft.com.

The advantage of Nslookup is that you can test the functionality and the quality of the information on a specific DNS server by specifying it on the command line.

Other Utilities Included with TCP/IP

> The following command-line utilities are included with TCP/IP:
>
> - Use Hostname to display your client's name
> - Use Ipconfig to display the IP configuration of your client
> - Use Netstat to display the network activity on your client

Introduction

When Windows Server 2003 is installed, it automatically includes the TCP/IP protocol, as well as numerous utilities that you can use to monitor TCP/IP and to check how well it is functioning.

The most commonly used utilities are described in the following paragraphs.

Use Hostname to display your client's name

The Hostname utility displays the host name that is assigned to your client. By default, the host name is the computer name of your client.

Use Ipconfig to display the IP configuration of your client

You can use the Ipconfig command-line utility both to display the current configuration of the installed IP stack on a networked computer and to refresh DHCP and DNS settings. Ipconfig will:

- Display current TCP/IP network configuration values.
- Update or release DHCP allocated leases.
- Display, register, or flush DNS names.

Ipconfig is most useful for managing computers that obtain an IP address automatically, such as by using DHCP or Automatic Private IP Addressing (APIPA).

Use Netstat to display the network activity on your client

Netstat displays information both about the current network connections of a client running TCP/IP and about the traffic generated by the various TCP/IP protocols. Use Netstat when you want to determine if a port is available or in use. The network connection listing displayed by netstat on a Windows Server 2003 computer appears as follows:

```
C:\>netstat

Active Connections

  Proto   Local Address        Foreign Address        State
  TCP     bottxp:990           localhost:3124         ESTABLISHED
  TCP     bottxp:999           localhost:3127         ESTABLISHED
  TCP     bottxp:1024          localhost:3040         ESTABLISHED
  TCP     bottxp:3040          localhost:1024         ESTABLISHED
  TCP     bottxp:3119          localhost:7438         ESTABLISHED
  TCP     bottxp:3120          localhost:5679         ESTABLISHED
  TCP     bottxp:3124          localhost:990          ESTABLISHED
  TCP     bottxp:3125          localhost:5678         ESTABLISHED
  TCP     bottxp:3126          localhost:5678         ESTABLISHED
  TCP     bottxp:3127          localhost:999          ESTABLISHED
  TCP     bottxp:5678          localhost:3125         ESTABLISHED
  TCP     bottxp:5678          localhost:3126         ESTABLISHED
  TCP     bottxp:5679          localhost:3120         ESTABLISHED
  TCP     bottxp:7438          localhost:3119         ESTABLISHED
  TCP     bottxp:3098          etcdaldc1:4092         ESTABLISHED
```

Using the Ping Utility to Test Connectivity to a Remote Host

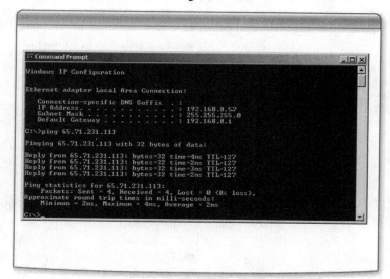

Introduction

The Ping utility and its variations are some of the most frequently used TCP/IP utilities. You can use Ping as your primary utility for isolating IP-level connectivity between two hosts. When it is used to isolate connectivity issues, Ping tests are done on successively more distant hosts until a failure is discovered. Use the following series of Ping commands to test connectivity between the local computer and a remote host.

Testing connectivity to a remote host

The following steps describe how to use the Ping utility to perform progressively more distant tests on your network connectivity.

1. Ping the loopback address—type **ping 127.0.0.1**

    Successfully pinging the loopback address verifies that TCP/IP is both installed on and correctly configured on the local client. If the loopback test fails, the IP stack is not responding. Lack of response can occur if the TCP drivers are corrupted, if the network adapter is not working, or if another service is interfering with IP. Open Event Viewer, and look for problems reported by Setup or by the TCP/IP service.

2. Ping the local client—type **ping <*IP address of local client*>**

    Successfully pinging the IP address of the local client verifies that the client was correctly added to the network. If you cannot successfully ping the local IP address after successfully pinging the loopback address, check that the local client's IP address is a valid IP address, check the routing table, and check the network adapter driver.

3. Ping the default gateway on the local computer—type
    ping <*IP address of the default gateway*>

    Successfully pinging the default gateway of the local client verifies both that the default gateway is functioning and that you can communicate with a local host on the local subnet. If you cannot successfully ping the default gateway after successfully pinging the local client, check the default gateway.

4. Ping the IP address of another computer or network device located on a remote network—type **ping** *<IP address of remote host>*

Successfully pinging the IP address of the remote host verifies that the local client can communicate with the remote host through a router. If the remote host is located across a high-delay link (such as a satellite link), try using the **-w** (wait) parameter to specify a longer time-out period than the default time-out of four seconds.

If you cannot successfully ping the remote host IP address after successfully pinging the default gateway, this can indicate that the remote host is not responding, or that there is a problem in the network hardware between the source host and the destination host. To rule out the possibility of a problem in the network hardware, ping a different remote host on the same subnet where the first remote host is located.

5. Ping the host name of another host on a remote network—type **ping** *<host name of remote host>*

Successfully pinging the name of a remote host verifies that ping can resolve the remote host name to an IP address. If you cannot successfully ping the remote host name after successfully pinging the IP address of the remote host, the problem is host name resolution, not network connectivity. When pinging the host name of the target host, ping attempts to resolve the name to an address (first through a DNS server, and next through a WINS server, if one is configured), and then attempts a local broadcast. Check TCP/IP properties to see whether the client has DNS server and WINS server addresses configured, either typed manually or assigned automatically. If DNS server and WINS server addresses are configured in TCP/IP properties, and if they appear when you type **ipconfig /all**, then try pinging the server addresses to ascertain whether they are accessible.

On a network that uses DNS for name resolution, if the name entered is not a fully qualified domain name (FQDN), the DNS name resolver appends the computer's domain name or names to generate the FQDN. Name resolution might fail if you do not use an FQDN for a remote name. These requests fail because the DNS name resolver appends the local domain suffix to a name that resides elsewhere in the domain hierarchy.

6. Temporarily turn off IPSec—retry all of the preceding ping commands.

If none of the preceding ping commands are successful, check whether IP Security (IPSec) is enabled. If IPSec is enabled locally, temporarily stop the IPSec Services service in the Services snap-in, and then try pinging again. If network connectivity between hosts works after you stop IPSec, ask the security administrator to troubleshoot the IPSec policy.

Note For more information about IPSec, see Module 8, "Securing Network Traffic by Using IPSec and Certificates," in Course 2277, *Implementing, Managing, and Maintaining a Microsoft Windows Server 2003 Network Infrastructure: Network Services.*

Interpreting Ping Error Messages

The following error messages generated by the Ping utility give you a great deal of information about your network connectivity:

- TTL expired in transit
- Destination host unreachable
- Request timed out
- Unknown host

Introduction

Each time you ping a host, ping will display a message showing the result, either a successful response or an error message. The type of error is a good clue as to the source of a connectivity problem.

TTL expired in transit

This message indicates that the number of hops required to reach the destination exceeds the TTL (time to live) set by the sending host to forward the packets. The default TTL value for Internet Control Message Protocol (ICMP) Echo Requests sent by Ping is 128. In some cases, this is not enough to travel the required number of links to a destination. You can increase the TTL by using the -i switch, up to a maximum of 255 links.

If increasing the TTL value fails to resolve the problem, the packets are being forwarded in a routing loop, a circular path among routers.

Use Tracert to track down the location of the routing loop, which appears as a repeated series of the same IP addresses in the Tracert report. Next, make an appropriate change to the routing tables, or inform the administrator of a remote router of the problem.

Destination host unreachable

This message indicates one of two problems: either the local client has no route to the desired destination, or a remote router reports that *it* has no route to the destination. The form of the message can distinguish the two problems. If the message is simply Destination Host Unreachable, then there is no route from the local client, and the packets to be sent were never put on the network. Use the Route utility to check the local routing table for either a direct route to the destination or a default gateway.

If the message is "Reply From <*IP address*>: Destination Host Unreachable," then the routing problem occurred at a remote router.

Request timed out

This message indicates that the Echo Reply messages were not received within the designated time-out period. By default, the Ping utility waits four seconds for each response to be returned before timing out. If the remote system pinged is across a high-delay link (such as a satellite link), responses might take longer to be returned. Use the **-w** (wait) switch to specify a longer time-out period.

To check for network congestion, simply increase the allowed latency by setting a higher wait time (such as 5000 milliseconds) by using the **-w** switch. Try to ping the destination again. If the request still times out, congestion is not the problem; an address resolution problem or a routing error is more likely the issue.

Unknown host

This error message appears as "Ping request could not find host <*host name*>. Please check the name and try again." It indicates that the requested host name cannot be resolved to its IP address; check that the name is entered correctly, and that the DNS servers can resolve it.

Variations on Ping

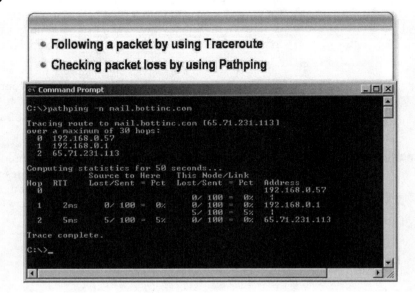

Introduction

Traceroute (tracert) is a variant of the Ping utility that displays the route that packets take to a destination, in addition to the usual Ping messages. Traceroute can show how far your packets are going before they run into a problem. Pathping combines features of both Ping and Traceroute to obtain additional information about router performance and link reliability that is not available to either of those tools.

Following a packet by using Traceroute

Because of the nature of IP routing, paths through an internetwork can change from minute to minute. Traceroute displays a list of the routers that are currently forwarding packets to a specified destination.

Traceroute uses ICMP Echo and Echo Reply messages in the same way as Ping does, but it modifies the messages by changing the value of the TTL field in the IP header. The TTL field is designed to prevent packets from getting caught in router loops that keep them circulating endlessly around the network. The computer generating the packet normally sets a relatively high value for the TTL field; on Windows systems, the default value is 128. Each router that processes the packet reduces the TTL value by one. If the TTL value reaches zero, the last router discards the packet and transmits an ICMP error message back to the original sender.

When you start Traceroute by using the tracert command with the name or IP address of a target computer, the utility generates its first set of Echo Request messages with TTL values of 1. When the messages arrive at the first router on their path, the router decrements their TTL values to 0, discards the packets, and reports the errors to the sender. The error messages contain the router's address, which Traceroute displays as the first hop in the path to the destination. Traceroute's second set of Echo Request messages use a TTL value of 2, causing the second router on the path to discard the packets and generate error messages. The Echo Request messages in the third set have a TTL value of 3, and so on. Each set of packets travels one hop farther than the previous set before causing a router to return error messages to the source. The list of routers displayed by Traceroute as the path to the destination is the result of these error messages.

Checking packet loss by using Pathping

Like Traceroute, Pathping discovers the path to a destination. Pathping sends multiple Echo Request messages to each router between a source and destination over a period of time and then computes results based on the packets returned from each router. Because Pathping displays the degree of packet loss at any given router or link, you can determine which routers or subnets might be having network problems. Pathping performs the equivalent of Traceroute by identifying which routers are on the path. It then pings all of the routers over a specified time period and computes statistics based on the value returned from each router.

The path data reported by Pathping includes:

- Information on the intermediate routers visited on the path.

- The round-trip time (RTT) value.

- Link loss information.

```
C:\Documents and Settings\Administrator>pathping microsoft.com

Tracing route to microsoft.com [207.46.249.27]
over a maximum of 30 hops:
  0  londonsbs [192.168.0.57]
  1  192.168.0.1
  2  adsl-65-71-231-118.dsl.rcsntx.swbell.net [65.71.231.118]
  3      *     dist1-vlan130.rcsntx.swbell.net
[151.164.162.130]
  4  bb1-g1-0.rcsntx.swbell.net [151.164.1.174]
  5      *     core1-6-0.crdltx.sbcglobal.net [151.164.240.66]
  6  core1-p11-0.crhnva.sbcglobal.net [151.164.243.218]
  7      *     bb1-p10-0.hrndva.sbcglobal.net [151.164.242.70]
  8  bb1-p6-0.pxvnva.sbcglobal.net [151.164.241.26]
  9      *     asn8075-microsoft.pxvnva.sbcglobal.net
[151.164.89.194]
 10      *     gig0-0.core1.was1.us.msn.net [207.46.33.101]
 11  gig4-2.edge2.ash1.us.msn.net [207.46.34.22]
 12  207.46.34.25
 13  207.46.33.61
 14  207.46.36.214
 15  207.46.155.13
 16      *         *         *
```

```
Computing statistics for 400 seconds...
                Source to Here   This Node/Link
Hop   RTT     Lost/Sent = Pct   Lost/Sent = Pct   Address
  0                                                londonsbs
[192.168.0.57]
                                 0/ 100 =  0%    |
  1    2ms     0/ 100 =  0%      0/ 100 =  0%    192.168.0.1
                                 0/ 100 =  0%    |
  2    14ms    1/ 100 =  1%      1/ 100 =  1%    adsl-65-71-231-
118.dsl.rcsntx.swbell.net [65.71.231.118]
                                 0/ 100 =  0%    |
  3    15ms    1/ 100 =  1%      1/ 100 =  1%    dist1-
vlan130.rcsntx.swbell.net [151.164.162.130]
                                 0/ 100 =  0%    |
  4    14ms    0/ 100 =  0%      0/ 100 =  0%    bb1-g1-
0.rcsntx.swbell.net [151.164.1.174]
                                 0/ 100 =  0%    |
  5    15ms    0/ 100 =  0%      0/ 100 =  0%    core1-6-
0.crdltx.sbcglobal.net [151.164.240.66]
                                 0/ 100 =  0%    |
  6    31ms    0/ 100 =  0%      0/ 100 =  0%    core1-p11-
0.crhnva.sbcglobal.net [151.164.243.218]
                                 0/ 100 =  0%    |
  7    30ms    0/ 100 =  0%      0/ 100 =  0%    bb1-p10-
0.hrndva.sbcglobal.net [151.164.242.70]
                                 0/ 100 =  0%    |
  8    31ms    0/ 100 =  0%      0/ 100 =  0%    bb1-p6-
0.pxvnva.sbcglobal.net [151.164.241.26]
                                 0/ 100 =  0%    |
  9    35ms    0/ 100 =  0%      0/ 100 =  0%    asn8075-
microsoft.pxvnva.sbcglobal.net [151.164.89.194]
                                 1/ 100 =  1%    |
 10    ---   100/ 100 =100%     99/ 100 = 99%    gig0-
0.core1.was1.us.msn.net [207.46.33.101]
                                 0/ 100 =  0%    |
 11    ---   100/ 100 =100%     99/ 100 = 99%    gig4-
2.edge2.ash1.us.msn.net [207.46.34.22]
                                 0/ 100 =  0%    |
 12    ---   100/ 100 =100%     99/ 100 = 99%    207.46.34.25
                                 0/ 100 =  0%    |
 13    ---   100/ 100 =100%     99/ 100 = 99%    207.46.33.61
                                 0/ 100 =  0%    |
 14    ---   100/ 100 =100%     99/ 100 = 99%    207.46.36.214
                                 0/ 100 =  0%    |
 15    62ms    1/ 100 =  1%      0/ 100 =  0%    207.46.155.13
                                99/ 100 = 99%    |
 16    ---   100/ 100 =100%      0/ 100 =  0%    londonsbs
[0.0.0.0]
```

Trace complete.

Features of the Network Connections Repair Option

> The Network Connections Repair Option can perform the following actions:
> - Broadcast DHCP lease renew
> - Flush the ARP cache
> - Flush the NetBIOS name cache
> - Re-register the client's name with a WINS server
> - Flush the DNS cache
> - Register a DNS name

Introduction

Network Connections Repair Link combines six of the most commonly used TCP/IP troubleshooting commands in one Windows utility.

Running Network Connections Repair Link

Network Connections Repair Link can be accessed in any of three ways:

- Right-click a network connection icon in the Network Connections folder, and then click **Repair**.

- Right-click the information balloon that appears in the system tray when your IP configuration becomes invalid, and then click **Repair**.

- In the **Status** dialog box, click the **Support** tab, and then click **Repair**.

When selecting a network connection, look in the left-hand column (if shown) for the **Repair this connection** link.

The following tasks are performed in the order listed:

Broadcast DHCP lease renew

This is the equivalent of a DHCP broadcast renewal at 87.5% of the lease time. This was chosen because it is far safer than actually doing first a DHCP release and then a DHCP renew. If a DHCP server is unavailable to renew the address, the client keeps its current address. If a new DHCP server comes online, the DHCP server can not acknowledge (NACK) the client and restart the lease process, potentially fixing a client's IP address problem.

Flush the ARP cache

Sometimes an ARP cache entry becomes outdated, and then communication cannot occur again until the bad ARP cache entry expires. It is also possible for a bad static ARP cache entry that never expires to have been placed on the client. The ARP cache is naturally flushed at 2 minute and 10 minute intervals, so this operation is considered safe.

Note If your network relies on static ARP cache entries, make sure that there is a way to reenter the ARP cache addresses after this tool is run.

Flush the NetBIOS name cache

Often the NetBIOS cache can have outdated entries, and then communication cannot occur. The **nbtstat –r** command clears the NetBIOS name cache and then reloads any NetBIOS name entries in the Lmhosts file with the #PRE flag.

Re-register the client's name with a WINS server

The **nbtstat –rr** command is the equivalent of re-registering the client's name with a WINS server. This can be very useful in isolating problems with NetBIOS name resolution.

Note   This task simply schedules the name refresh with the operating system; it does not check to determine whether the refresh was successful.

Flush the DNS cache

This task flushes any old or bad DNS cache entries from memory. This can be very useful in isolating problems with DNS name resolution.

Register a DNS name

This task re-registers the client's DNS name with a DNS dynamic update server.

How to Use Network Diagnostics to Gather System Information

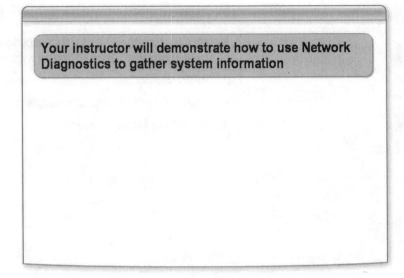

Your instructor will demonstrate how to use Network Diagnostics to gather system information

Introduction

Network Diagnostics performs a series of tests to gather important information that can help you isolate the causes of network-related issues. Depending on the options you select, it checks your system for network connectivity and whether your network-related programs and services are running. It also gathers basic information about your computer.

Note Most of the utilities that you need to help you isolate network problems are automatically installed when you install Windows Server 2003. You can install Network Diagnostics and many additional Windows Server 2003 support tools from the operating system CD when you need them. After you install the support tools, Netdiag.exe appears in the C:\Program Files\Support Tools folder.

Using Network Diagnostics

Unlike most of the other network utilities, Network Diagnostics is a Windows-based utility rather than a command-line utility.

▶ **To scan your computer using Network Diagnostics**

1. Click **Start**, and then click **Help and Support**.

2. Click **Tools**.

3. Click **Help and Support Center Tools**.

4. Click **Network Diagnostics**.

5. Click **Set scanning options**.

   The list of scanning options appears.

6. Select all available options.

7. Click **Scan your system**.

   Network Diagnostics scans your system to gather information about your hardware, software, and network connections and presents the information as a report in the window.

Features of the Netsh Command

> Netsh can manage various network services with
> commands that are separated into different contexts:
>
> - Netsh contexts
> - Availability of Netsh commands
> - Accessing Netsh contexts

Introduction

Netsh is a command-line scripting interface that runs from a Command Prompt that contains a variety of contexts from which you can type commands. The context is indicated by the netsh prompt, which by default is **netsh>**. The Netsh commands are specifically for managing and monitoring network services such as DHCP, WINS, TCP/IP, and IPSec.

Netsh contexts

Each Netsh context contains the features for managing a specific related set of networking functions. A *Netsh context* is a state in which Netsh accepts commands related to a specific set of functions.

Availability of Netsh commands

Some commands are available only within a specific context. Some commands are available not only in the context shown in the command lists, but also in all subcontexts (if any exist) below that context.

Global commands work in all contexts. Some of these, like the help command, produce different results in different contexts. Others, such as add helper (used to load a new Helper dynamic link library [DLL] into Netsh) always produce the same result in Netsh, no matter which context you are working in.

Accessing Netsh contexts

Contexts are arranged in a hierarchy. At the top of the context hierarchy is the Netsh root context. The following table lists the contexts and subcontexts in hierarchical order, in addition to the Helper DLL that provides each context. The **show helper** command in Netsh displays this information.

Context	Subcontext	Subcontext
aaaa		
diag		
dhcp		
	server	
		mscope
		scope
interface		
	ip	
ras		
	aaaa	
	appletalk	
	ip	
routing		
	ip	
		autodhcp
		dnsproxy
		igmp
		nat
		ospf
		relay
		rip
		routerdiscovery
wins		
	server	

You can change to another context by typing the name of the context (for example, **interface**) at the **netsh>** prompt. Your command prompt changes to match the context entered. If you are already in a context, you can go to a subcontext by typing the name of the subcontext (for example, **ip**).

Contexts are provided by Helper DLLs. If you cannot access a specific context, follow the instructions in Helper DLLs to make sure that the files for that context are loaded.

How to Access Netsh Contexts

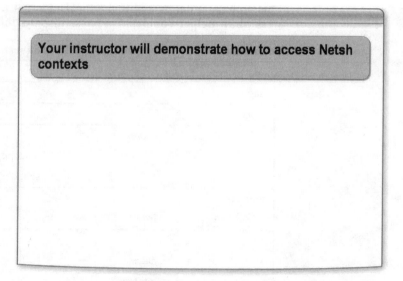

Your instructor will demonstrate how to access Netsh contexts

Introduction

Related Netsh commands are grouped into contexts. In order to run a Netsh command, you must first invoke Netsh and then change to the context that contains the desired command.

Using Netsh command contexts

To access the Netsh command contexts:

1. Open a command prompt window, and enter **netsh** at the command prompt as shown:

    ```
    C:\>netsh
    ```

    Netsh becomes the active command line interpreter, or *shell*, and the command prompt changes to:

    ```
    netsh>
    ```

    At this point, you are in the root context of Netsh, and you can use a limited number of Netsh global commands.

2. To change to one of the Netsh contexts, such as the IP context under the Routing context, enter the context path at the Netsh prompt as shown:

    ```
    netsh>routing ip
    ```

    Netsh routing ip becomes the active context, and the command prompt changes to:

    ```
    netsh routing ip>
    ```

3. Enter a command that is available in the current context (such as the **set interface** command, which sets the specified IP interface mode):

```
netsh routing ip>set interface name="Beta Network"
state=enable
```

4. To move up the context hierarchy, type **..** (two periods), and then press ENTER.

How to Use the Netsh Command to Configure a Network Interface Adapter

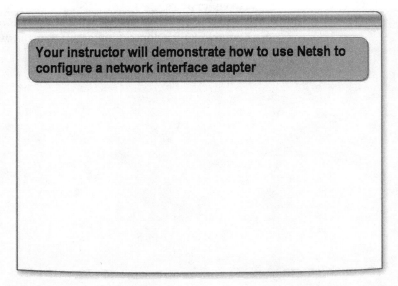

Your instructor will demonstrate how to use Netsh to configure a network interface adapter

Introduction

The Netsh command provides you with the ability to change between static and dynamic IP addresses on a network interface adapter.

Using Netsh to configure a network interface adapter for static IP

To use the Netsh command to configure a network interface adapter to use a static IP address:

1. Open a command prompt.

2. To verify that you are currently using DHCP on your computer, type **ipconfig /all** and then press ENTER. The DHCP enabled=Yes message is displayed.

3. At the command prompt, type **netsh interface ip set address name="***interface_name***" source=static addr=192.168.***x.y*** mask=255.255.255.0** (where *interface_name* is the name of your local area connection, *x* is the network number, and *y* is the student number provided by your instructor), and then press ENTER.

Using Netsh to configure a network interface adapter for dynamic IP

To use the Netsh command to configure a network interface adapter to use a dynamic IP address:

1. Open a command prompt.

2. Verify that you are now using a static IP address on your computer by typing **ipconfig /all** and then pressing ENTER. The DHCP enabled=No message is displayed.

3. At the command prompt, type **netsh interface ip set address name="***interface_name***" source=dhcp** and then press ENTER.

4. Verify that your network interface is configured to obtain an IP address automatically by typing **ipconfig /all** and pressing ENTER. The DHCP enabled=Yes message is displayed.

Lab A: Isolating Common Connectivity Issues

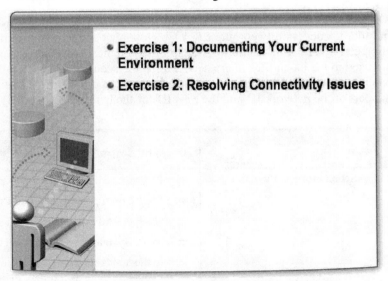

Objectives	After completing this lab, you will be able to isolate common connectivity issues using a troubleshooting flow chart.
Prerequisites	Before working on this lab, you must have knowledge of TCP/IP configuration settings on a client computer running a Windows operating system.
Scenario	This lab consists of four scenarios. Each scenario outlines a connectivity issue that you will need to resolve. You will use the Network Connectivity Job Aid to isolate client connectivity issues. In each scenario, you will execute a batch file that will introduce an issue into the system. You will then work through a series of steps to isolate and fix the issue.

Note To view the Problem Isolation Flow Chart, see Appendix C.

Lab answers	The detailed steps for this lab—along with the answers to the questions—are found at the end of this lab.
Estimated time to complete this lab: 60 minutes	

Exercise 0
Lab Setup

In order to successfully complete this lab, you must add two environment variables to your computer and rename the network adapter icon in network connections. The environment variables are used in the batch files to create and undo the scenarios. For example, to reset your IP address, a batch file is run that has your IP address as part of a command. The environment variables supply the part of the network ID and the host ID for the batch file.

Tasks	Detailed steps
1. Set environment variables.	a. Log on as administrator with a password of **P@ssw0rd**. b. Click **Start**, point to **Control Panel**, and then click **System**. c. Click the **Advanced** tab, and then click **Environment Variables**. d. In the **System Variables** box, click **New**. e. In the **Variable name** box, type **mochost** and then, in the **Variable value** box, type the number of your host address according to the following table. f. Click **OK**. g. Repeat steps c through e, using **mocnet** as the variable name and the network number *x* (where *x* is the number of the classroom) as the variable value.
Note: The environment variables are single integers, not IP addresses. The mochost environment variable is an integer from 11 to 34 according to the table below. The mocnet variable is also a single integer that corresponds to the classroom number, for example 5.	
1. (*continued*)	h. To close the **Environment Variables** dialog box, click **OK**. i. To close the **System Properties** dialog box, click **OK**.
2. Name your LAN connection moclan.	a. Click **Start**, point to **Control Panel**, right-click **Network Connections**, and then click **Open**. b. Right-click your primary network connection, and then click **Rename**. c. Type **moclan** and then press ENTER.
3. Enable DHCP.	a. Click **Start**, point to **Control Panel**, point to **Network Connections**, and then click **MOCLAN**. The **MOCLAN Status** dialog box appears. b. Click **Properties**. The MOCLAN Properties dialog box appears. c. Click **Internet Protocol (TCP/IP)**, and then click **Properties**. The Internet Protocol (TCP/IP) Properties dialog box appears. d. Click **Obtain an IP address automatically**. e. Click **Obtain DNS server address automatically**, and then click **OK**. f. To close the **MOCLAN Properties** dialog box, click **Close**. g. To close the **MOCLAN Status** dialog box, click **Close**.

4.	Close all windows.	▪ Close all windows and log off.
5.	Log on as *Computer*User	▪ Log on as NWTRADERS*Computer*User (where *Computer* is the name of your computer).

Computer Name	MOCHOST Value
Vancouver	11
Denver	12
Perth	13
Brisbane	14
Lisbon	15
Bonn	16
Lima	17
Santiago	18
Bangalore	19
Singapore	20
Casablanca	21
Tunis	22
Acapulco	23
Miami	24
Auckland	25
Suva	26
Stockholm	27
Moscow	28
Caracas	29
Montevideo	30
Manila	31
Tokyo	32
Khartoum	33
Nairobi	34

Exercise 1
Documenting Your Current Environment

As you run the scripts to introduce scenarios, you may be changing the configuration settings of your computer in order to solve the issue. At the end of each scenario, you will reset your computer. Document your configuration settings by completing the following table, and refer to this table to verify that settings are correctly configured after resetting your computer.

Item	Configuration
Your network number	1
Your computer's IP address	192.168.1.50
Your default gateway	.1.200
Your primary DNS Server	.1.200
Your secondary DNS Server	
Your WINS Server	.1.200
Your computer's NetBT node type	Hybrid
Remote address (an address outside your local network)	

Exercise 2
Resolving Connectivity Issues

This lab consists of four scenarios. Each scenario outlines a connectivity issue that you will need to resolve. You will use the Problem Isolation Flow Chart in Appendix C to isolate client connectivity issues. In each scenario, you will execute a batch file that will introduce an issue into the system. You will then work through a series of steps to isolate and fix the issue.

Scenario 1: Resolving a Request Timed Out Connectivity Issue

A customer has logged a helpdesk request stating that he cannot access any network resources. He is receiving a Request timed out error. You are working at the user's computer to isolate the connectivity issue and either resolve it yourself or escalate it to a system engineer.

Tasks	Specific Instructions
1. Introduce the problem.	▪ Using administrator credentials, run **c:\moc\2276\labfiles\s1.bat**.
2. Isolate the issue.	a. Use the Ping utility to send an echo request to localhost. b. Ping London. c. Verify your own IP configuration.
❓ After you pinged localhost, did the TCP/IP stack function properly? *yes*	
❓ After you pinged London, did you receive a successful reply? *yes*	
❓ When you verified your own IP configuration, was it correct? If not, what was the issue? 	
3. Correct the problem.	▪ Navigate to **Network Connections** in Control Panel, use moclan and correct the problem.
4. Reset the computer configuration.	▪ Using administrator credentials, run **c:\moc\2276\labfiles\r1.bat**.

Scenario 2: User Cannot Access Any Network Resources

A user complains that he cannot access any network resource. He mentioned seeing a dialog box, stating something about a duplicate IP address on the network.

Tasks	Specific Instructions
1. Introduce the problem.	▪ Using administrator credentials, run **c:\moc\2276\labfiles\s2.bat**.
2. Isolate issues associated with this scenario.	a. Review the IP configuration information by using **ipconfig /all**. b. Determine whether DHCP is enabled. $\gamma^{2/\mathcal{R}}$ c. Verify that the ARP cache lists a network interface adapter. d. Isolate the issue.
❓	Is the adapter configured for DHCP? _____
❓	What is the value of the IP address and the subnet mask? _____ _____
❓	When you verify the ARP, what is the response? _____ _____
❓	What is the issue? _____ _____
3. Correct the problem.	▪ Using moclan, correct the problem.
4. Reset the computer configuration.	▪ Using administrator credentials, run **c:\moc\2276\labfiles\r2.bat**.

Scenario 3: Partial Access to Network Resources

A user at a remote office has only partial access to the network. She can access a coworker's shared folder files the London computer is inaccessible to her. You are at the user's computer to isolate the connectivity issue and either fix it yourself, or escalate it to a systems engineer. For this scenario, you are working to restore connectivity to the London computer.

Tasks	Specific Instructions
1. Introduce the problem.	▪ Using administrator credentials, run **c:\moc\2276\labfiles\s3.bat**.
2. Isolate issues associated with this scenario.	a. Ping localhost. b. Ping London. c. Run Nslookup to query the London computer.
❓ Can you ping the localhost? Did you receive an answer? *yes, yes*	
❓ Can you ping London? What is the response? What is the displayed address for London? *NO, Request timed out 1.4.1.4*	
❓ Was the nslookup query on the London computer successful? *No*	
❓ What is the most likely problem?	
3. Correct the problem.	
4. Reset the computer configuration.	▪ Using administrator credentials, run **c:\moc\2276\labfiles\r3.bat**.

Scenario 4: Unable to Access Host by IP Address

A user in the local office is having difficulty accessing the London computer. The user is unable to print to the print device connected to the London computer and cannot access any of the files located in shared folders on the London computer. In this scenario, you are working to restore connectivity to the London computer.

Tasks	Specific Instructions
1. Introduce the problem.	▪ Using administrator credentials, run **c:\moc\2276\labfiles\s4.bat**.
2. Isolate issues associated with this scenario.	a. Ping localhost. b. Ping London. c. Ping 192.168.*x*.200.
? Can you ping the localhost successfully? Is TCP/IP functioning properly? _Yes_	
? Can you ping London successfully? What does the output of the ping indicate? _Yes 0% loss_	
? Can you ping 192.168.*x*.200? What is the reply?	
? What is the issue?	
3. Correct the problem.	
4. Reset the computer configuration.	▪ Using administrator credentials, run **c:\moc\2276\labfiles\r4.bat**.

Course Evaluation

Your evaluation of this course will help Microsoft understand the quality of your learning experience.

To complete a course evaluation, go to http://www.CourseSurvey.com.

Microsoft will keep your evaluation strictly confidential and will use your responses to improve your future learning experience.

Appendix C: Problem Isolation Flow Chart

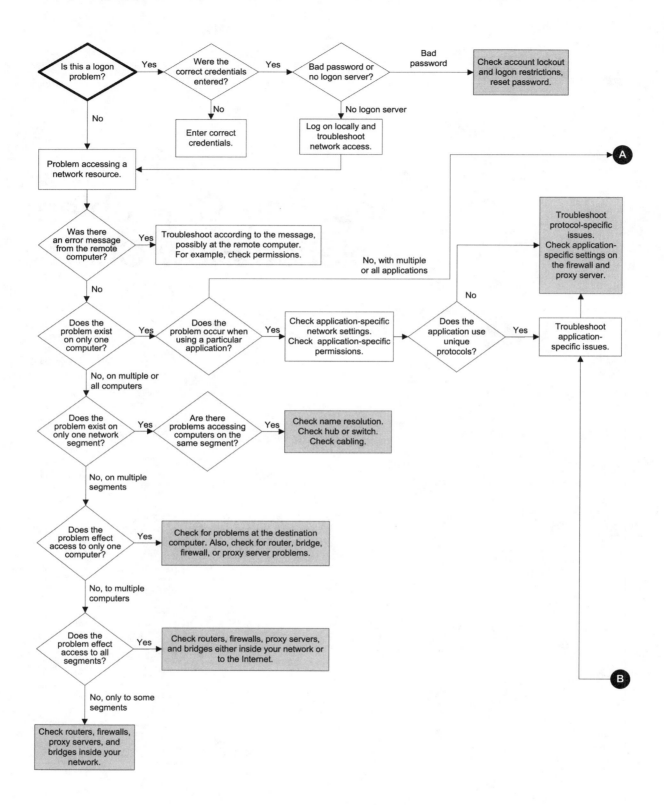

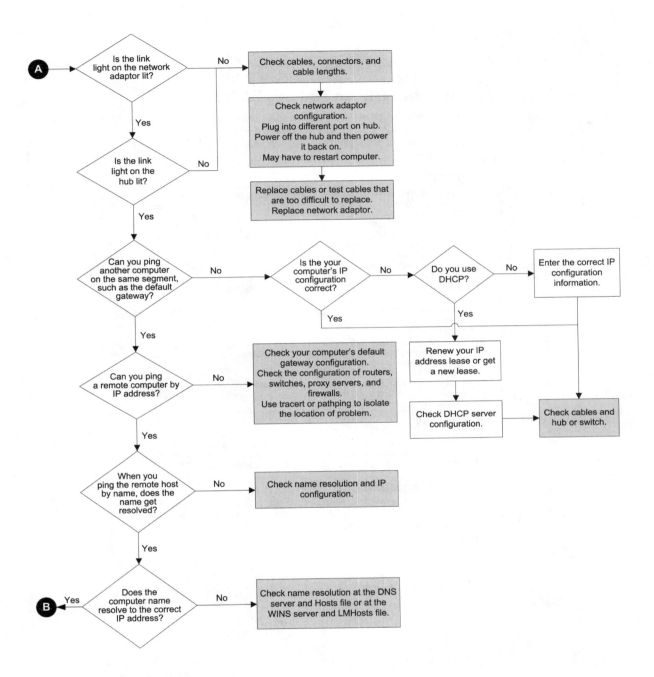

Microsoft® Windows® Server 2003 Enterprise Edition 180-Day Evaluation

The software included in this kit is intended for evaluation and deployment planning purposes only. If you plan to install the software on your primary machine, it is recommended that you back up your existing data prior to installation.

System requirements

To use Microsoft Windows Server 2003 Enterprise Edition, you need:
- Computer with 550 MHz or higher processor clock speed recommended; 133 MHz minimum required; Intel Pentium/Celeron family, or AMD K6/Athlon/Duron family, or compatible processor (Windows Server 2003 Enterprise Edition supports up to eight CPUs on one server)
- 256 MB of RAM or higher recommended; 128 MB minimum required (maximum 32 GB of RAM)
- 1.25 to 2 GB of available hard-disk space*
- CD-ROM or DVD-ROM drive
- Super VGA (800 × 600) or higher-resolution monitor recommended; VGA or hardware that supports console redirection required
- Keyboard and Microsoft Mouse or compatible pointing device, or hardware that supports console redirection

Additional items or services required to use certain Windows Server 2003 Enterprise Edition features:
- For Internet access:
  - Some Internet functionality may require Internet access, a Microsoft Passport account, and payment of a separate fee to a service provider; local and/or long-distance telephone toll charges may apply
  - High-speed modem or broadband Internet connection
- For networking:
  - Network adapter appropriate for the type of local-area, wide-area, wireless, or home network to which you wish to connect, and access to an appropriate network infrastructure; access to third-party networks may require additional charges

Note: To ensure that your applications and hardware are Windows Server 2003–ready, be sure to visit **www.microsoft.com/windowsserver2003**.

* Actual requirements will vary based on your system configuration and the applications and features you choose to install. Additional available hard-disk space may be required if you are installing over a network. For more information, please see **www.microsoft.com/windowsserver2003**.

Uninstall instructions

This time-limited release of Microsoft Windows Server 2003 Enterprise Edition will expire 180 days after installation. If you decide to discontinue the use of this software, you will need to reinstall your original operating system. You may need to reformat your drive.

Microsoft®

Notes

Notes

Notes

Notes

Notes

Notes

Notes

Notes

Notes

Notes

Notes

Notes